THE MAKING OF
Moll Flanders

ANTHONY HAYWARD

THE MAKING OF
Moll Flanders

HEADLINE

In association with
GRANADA TELEVISION

ALSO BY ANTHONY HAYWARD

Who's Who on Television
Coronation Street — Celebrating 30 Years (editor and co-author)
Phantom — Michael Crawford Unmasked
Street Cred
The Who's Who of Soap Operas
TV Unforgettables (with Deborah Hayward)
Annie's Song: My Life & Emmerdale (with Sheila Mercier)

First published in 1996 by
HEADLINE BOOK PUBLISHING

10 9 8 7 6 5 4 3 2 1

ISBN 0 7472 7742 7

Printed and bound in Italy
by Canale & C.S.p.A.
Designed by Peter Ward

HEADLINE BOOK PUBLISHING
A division of Hodder Headline PLC
338 Euston Road
London NW1 3BH

List of Contents

Acknowledgements

For the help they extended me during my research for this book, I would like to thank David Lascelles, David Attwood, Gub Neal, Susie Conklin, Stephen Fineren, Trisha Biggar, Sue Milton, Ivan Strasburg, Vinny Fahy, Mark Springer, Alex Kingston, Daniel Craig, Ian Driver, Christopher Fulford, John Savident, James Fleet and Nicola Walker, as well as the rest of the cast and crew who allowed me access throughout the filming of *Moll Flanders*.

ANTHONY HAYWARD

The publishers would also like to thank the following for providing photographs: Harry Bluntlett; Bolton Museum & Art Gallery; Bourne United Charities; Chorley Arts & Museum Service; Andrew Davies; Kathryn de Belle; Tony Evans/Lindford-Bridgeman; Stephen Fineren; Haddon Hall, Bakewell, Derbyshire/Hedgerow Publishing; Hoghton Tower Limited; Governors, Lord Leycester Hospital; Grimsthorpe and Drummond Castle Trust Ltd; Mike Lawn; Neil Marland; Sally Miles; Helen Moran; National Trust Photographic Library; Scope Pictures; South West News Service; Tatton Park; *Western Daily Press.*

Cast

MOLL FLANDERS	Alex Kingston
JEMMY	Daniel Craig
GAOLER	James Bowers
MOLL'S MOTHER	Nicola Kingston
JUDGE (*Episode 1*)	Geoffrey Beevers
LITTLE MOLL	Lucy Evans
GYPSY	Antony Bessick
MR RICHARDSON	Struan Rodger
MRS FAIRLEY	Chrissie Cotterill
PARISH OFFICER	Peter Jonfield
MAGISTRATE	Neville Phillips
MRS RICHARDSON	Maureen O'Brien
ROWLAND	Colin Buchanan
ROBIN	Ian Driver
MARIA	Caroline Harker
EMILY	Dawn McDaniel
MR BAGGOT	Ken McDonald
MRS BAGGOT	Mary Healey
LANDLORD OF	
THE GOLDEN COCK	Jeff Nuttall
PRIEST AT FUNERAL	Philip Fox
ESTELLA	Victoria Scarborough
CAPTAIN STEPHENS	James Larkin
DANIEL DAWKINS	Christopher Fulford
ACTOR 1 (*Episode 1*)	Michael Johnson
ACTOR 2 (*Episode 1*)	Andrew Mayor
OLD WOMAN AT MINT	Evie Garratt
GENT AT MINT	Roger Ashton-Griffiths
FAT SEA CAPTAIN	Roger Morlidge
THIN SEA CAPTAIN	Sam Halpenny
LEMUEL	Tom Ward
MRS GOLIGHTLY	Diana Rigg
LANCASTER INNKEEPER	Bill Thomas
MRS SEAGRAVE	Trevyn McDowell
CAPTAIN O'MALLEY	Guy Scantlebury
CATHOLIC PRIEST	Anthony O'Donnell
STABLE BOY	Matthew O'Neil

MR BLAND	James Fleet
CLERGYMAN IN COACH	John Savident
ELDERLY LADY IN COACH	Anna Welsh
CHEEKY SERVING GIRL	Alison Lomas
MRS RIORDAN	Patti Love
MRS BLAND	Catherine Keis
LANDLORD AT WARE	Tony Milner
SERVANT GIRL	Anya Phillips
MR MEIKELJOHN	Milton Johns
LUCY DIVER	Nicola Walker
DANCING SCHOOL GIRL	Jenna Hodges
ACTOR 1 (*Episode 4*)	Lucy Fitzmaurice
ACTOR 2 (*Episode 4*)	Claire Keppie
FOP AT THEATRE	Jonathan Weir
JUDGE (*Episode 4*)	Brian Rawlinson
TYBURN PRIEST	Will Tacy
FAT MAN AT TYBURN	Irving Czechowicz
SIR RICHARD GREGORY	Ronald Fraser
ABIGAIL	Ruth Mitchell
MASTER DENISTON	Dallas Campbell
CONSTABLE	David Burston
PRISONER WITH RAT	Dave Norman
SWELL MOB WOMAN	Elisabeth Skelton
ANNIE	Caroline Trowbridge
CLERK OF COURT	Jeff Robert

PRODUCTION TEAM

DIRECTOR	David Attwood
PRODUCER	David Lascelles
EXECUTIVE PRODUCER	Gub Neal
WRITER	Andrew Davies, from the book by Daniel Defoe
SCRIPT EDITOR	Susie Conklin
PRODUCTION EXECUTIVE	Craig McNeil
CASTING DIRECTORS	Gail Stevens and Andy Prior
DESIGNER	Stephen Fineren
COSTUME DESIGNER	Trisha Biggar
MAKE-UP DESIGNER	Sue Milton

Director of Photography	Ivan Strasburg BSc
Editor	Edward Mansell
Music	Mark Springer and Sarah Sarhandi
Production Supervisor	Bill Leather
Production Manager	Bill Shephard
Location Managers	Mick Graham and Peter Cotton
Production Co-ordinator	Glenys Bell
Production Secretary	Dominique Molloy
1st Assistant Director	Vinny Fahy
2nd Assistant Director	Claire McCourt
3rd Assistant Director	Simon Turner
Floor Runners	Liz Reeve and Emily Lascelles
Sound Recordist	Nick Steer
Boom Operator	Ben Brooks
Script Supervisor	Helen Moran
Camera Operator	Andrew Stephen
Focus Puller	Andrew MacDonnel
Clapper/Loader	Steve Woods
Lighting Gaffer	Dave Ratcliffe
Electricians	Len Holt, Stuart Grant and Gordon Craig
Art Directors	Alan Price and Tim Farmer
Assistant Art Director	Nick Wilkinson
Construction Manager	Brian Eatough
Props	Peter Moran and Peter O'Rourke
Assistant Costume Designer	Lucy Wright
Dressers	Alex Cauldfield, Derek Rowe and Roy Charters
Make-up Assistants	Emma Ferguson and Jane Tyler
Alex Kingston's Make-up	Claire Heron
Sound Editors	John Senior and Mark Briscoe
Dubbing Mixer	John Whitworth
Graphics	Phil Buckley
Choreography	Carolyn Choa
Horse-master	Peter Wight
Animals	Pam Weaver
Stunts	Nick Powell and Nick Wilkinson

INTRODUCTION

DEEP IN THE Lancashire countryside on an overcast day in May, a stagecoach stands in a ravine in the middle of a forest. Masked highwaymen ride down a bank on horseback and tell the driver and his mate to drop their guns, then they order those inside to get out, line them up and take all their valuables. 'Do you consent to be searched, madam?' asks the gang's leader of the handsome, beautifully dressed woman at the end of the line. 'Under protest, sir,' she replies, with a broadening smile and a glint in her eye. The rascal then tells everyone to turn round and escorts the woman to a spot next to a stream.

'Cut!' shouts the director, and another scene is completed in Granada Television's costume drama *Moll Flanders*. Filming has already taken place at some of England's finest historic locations, from the National Trust's most popular property, Tatton Park, in Cheshire, to the famous timber-framed architecture of nearby Little Moreton Hall, and one of Lancashire's oldest manor houses, Smithills Hall.

The colourful costumes span the seventeenth century, one of change for women but even greater change for men, with the sombre colours and covered-up flesh of the Puritan period giving way to the great decoration and flamboyance of the Restoration era.

Costume drama has returned to television in recent years, but Granada Television did not simply want to adapt another nineteenth-century novel, which has become the fashion. Instead, the ITV company went back to the era of Daniel Defoe, best known as the writer of *Robinson Crusoe*, but also a noted pamphleteer at the turn of the seventeenth century, and dubbed the father of modern journalism.

Moll Flanders gave Granada the recipe for a historical costume drama-cum-saucy romp, four hours of television filled with beautiful costumes and locations, and a story of a spirited orphan who is seduced at an early age and marries five times, before entering a life of crime that leads to the gallows. The producer, David Lascelles, and adapter, Andrew Davies, also saw many parallels between *Moll Flanders* — considered to be one of the first social novels — and modern-day Britain, with divisions in society forcing those at the lower end to make very stark choices.

This book looks behind the scenes to reveal how *Moll Flanders* came to the screen, from the earliest decision to commission the script, to the set design, location-hunting and task of finding or creating 1,500 costumes of the era, as well as filming and editing.

CHAPTER ONE

FROM DANIEL DEFOE TO ANDREW DAVIES

The Fortunes and Misfortunes of the Famous Moll Flanders, Etc, who was Born at Newgate, and during a Life of continu'd Variety for Threescore Years, besides her Childhood, was Twelve Year a Whore, five times a Wife (whereof once to her own Brother), Twelve Year a Thief, Eight Year a Transported Felon in Virginia, at last grew Rich, liv'd Honest, and died a Penitent. Written from her own Memorandums.

— Complete title of Daniel Defoe's novel, 1722

Moll Flanders, thief and whore, the things she has done would chill you to the bone, I thank you, and you shall hear them all from her own lips, five times married, ladies and gentlemen, and once to her own brother. She'll show you all, if she's in the mood, aye, fornication, robbery, rape and murder, crowd up close, there, thank you, Sir . . .

— Gaoler in Andrew Davies's adaptation, 1996

DANIEL DEFOE's tale of the orphan who led a colourful life of romance and crime in seventeenth-century England — and across the water in the tobacco plantations of Virginia, to which her mother had been transported after being convicted of theft — has been adapted for the screen surprisingly few times. The story has all the lurid ingredients of a screen classic, following the life of a girl who lives with gypsies before being taken in by the Mayor of Colchester and his family, marrying five times — once unwittingly to her own brother, which she discovers when she finally meets her mother in America — and turning to a life of crime when there is no other way to make ends meet.

Film director Terence Young made *The Amorous Adventures of Moll Flanders* in the sixties as a bawdy romp starring Kim Novak, who gave a performance of great gusto as the heroine, supported by such well-known character players as Angela Lansbury, Leo McKern, George Sanders, Peter Butterworth and Dandy Nichols. Ten years later, in 1975, BBC2 made *Moll Flanders*, a long-forgotten television production featuring Julia Foster, with Ian Ogilvy and Kenneth Haigh among the actors playing her husbands. Outrageous director Ken Russell even planned his own film version but eventually abandoned the project.

The varying fortunes of Moll Flanders (Alex Kingston) echo those of author Daniel Defoe, who himself was imprisoned at Newgate.

After her mother is sentenced to transportation, Little Moll (Lucy Evans) is handed from one family to another, then lives with gypsies.

It was 1996 before the lusty heroine returned to the screen, with film and television versions coming out in the same year. In the summer, cinemas screened the American production *Moll Flanders*, filmed in Ireland and starring Robin Wright as Moll, with a cast that included Morgan Freeman, Stockard Channing, John Lynch, former *Casualty* star Brenda Fricker and *Band of Gold* actress Geraldine James. The film was written and directed by Pen Densham, who scripted *Robin Hood – Prince of Thieves*, but he set it in the eighteenth century – when the original book was published, but a century after the story was set – and made the character a mix of Defoe's Moll and other eighteenth-century women living in a world of turmoil.

Granada Television followed the original more faithfully with its £3.1 million production on the ITV network, heading the channel's autumn drama line-up. This came in the wake of the rebirth of classic serials on television, with *Middlemarch* and *Pride and Prejudice* both gaining critical acclaim during the previous two years. Granada's production had been thought of even before those came to the screen, but it was their success that undoubtedly helped the ITV company to get backing for its plans from the rest of the network.

Back in 1993, while Gub Neal – best known as the creator of *Cracker* and now Granada's controller of drama – was a producer with the company, he was discussing with the then controller of drama, Sally Head, programme proposals to put to the network. 'I mentioned that there had been a conspicuous lack of any sizeable classic drama on the network for some time,' recalls Gub, 'and she was bemoaning the fact that it was getting increasingly difficult to get commissions through.

'Anyway, I spoke to my script editor, Catriona McKenzie, who is now head of development, and she went off on a reading spree and decided it would be good to tackle something that had not been done for a little while. She came up with *Moll Flanders*, which had an upbeat quality that might be useful to ITV. It was, broadly speaking, quite vulgar and had the appeal that could be done like a *Tom Jones* work rather than a rarefied Jane Austen. It was felt it would be quite a good romp.'

Defoe had published his original story in 1722, at the age of sixty-two, and in it he must have drawn on some of his own experiences and feelings, for he had himself given up a planned career in the Presbyterian ministry to become a merchant, travelling throughout Europe, but found that misfortune continually followed him. 'No man has tasted differing fortunes more,' he wrote. 'And thirteen times I have been rich and poor.' He was declared bankrupt once and, as a writer of political pamphlets, faced fines and even imprisonment at Newgate, where Moll's life began and she later awaited her execution.

It was only in the twelve years leading up to his death in 1731 that Defoe became a noted novelist. *Robinson Crusoe* was published in 1719 and *The Fortunes and Misfortunes of the Famous Moll Flanders* came out three years later. These were the books that were to ensure his name lived on beyond that of the political activist he had been for much of his life, serving both the Tories and the Whigs, with 560 books, journals and pamplets to his credit.

His novels featured people facing struggle. The heroine of *Moll Flanders* spends most of her life picking herself up off the floor. Born in Newgate Prison, after her mother was arrested for petty theft, which leads to her transportation to Virginia, Moll is passed from one family to another until she goes to live with gypsies, then has the good fortune to be taken in by the Mayor of Colchester and his family, and this helps to fulfil her previously unlikely hopes of becoming a 'gentlewoman', although she finds herself having to help the servants to pay her way.

Love enters Moll's life when the Mayor's elder son falls for her, promising to marry her when he comes to inherit his father's estate, for he would be cut off without a penny if he married out of his class. But that will be many years away and, in the meantime, the couple keep their love a secret. Indeed, it is the Mayor's younger son who declares to all his love for Moll. She is heartbroken when her real lover dumps her by suggesting that she accepts his brother's hand in marriage. Worried about losing them both and being turned out on the streets, Moll agrees.

After five years of a loveless marriage and giving birth to two children, her husband dies and Moll heads for London with a small fortune and a desire to marry – on her own terms. So begins a trek through four more marriages – including the love of her life, Jemmy – and a time of such poverty that Moll joins the thieves on the streets of London to make a living.

Towards the end of 1993, Granada commissioned novelist Deborah Moggach – best known for books such as *Close to Home* and *To Have and to Hold* – to write the adaptation. 'She did a very good first hour,' recalls

The Mayor of Colchester, Mr Richardson (Struan Rodger), and his family take in Moll as 'almost one of the family' after she runs away from the gypsies.

Gub Neal, 'although it wasn't quite racy enough. We felt she had been a bit reverential with the book – her script felt filmic and not particularly picaresque. Then, Deborah went through a personal tragedy when her boyfriend died, and we felt it was an appropriate moment to ask her whether she wanted to set it aside and think about doing something else.'

It was then that Granada approached Andrew Davies, a former lecturer in English at Warwick University, who had become one of television's top writers, with original programmes such as two series of *A Very Peculiar Practice* and the one-off drama *Ball-Trap on the Côte Sauvage* under his belt. Davies's first television success had actually come with the children's series *Marmalade Atkins*, but he was also in demand for his adaptations of books such as *To Serve Them All My Days*, *Diana*, *Mother Love*, the *House of Cards* trilogy, *Anglo-Saxon Attitudes* and *The Old Devils*. Granada contacted Andrew after he had finished adapting George Eliot's *Middlemarch* for the BBC. He had previously written the script for the BBC's adaptation of Jane Austen's *Pride and Prejudice*, although that came to the screen after *Middlemarch*.

But first Granada had to persuade Andrew that he should take on the commission. 'Sally Head had worked with him before and was keen to do so again,' says Gub Neal. 'I sent the book off to Andrew for him to re-read, and his initial reaction was, "I'm not sure how I'd make a drama out of it."'

Andrew admits he was initially unsure about getting involved in the project. 'I was reluctant,' he says. 'It wasn't one book I would say yes to straight away. I knew it pretty well, having taught it at university, but I had not read it for years and years. I remembered it as a pretty funny, ramshackle sort of book. It doesn't have the kind of classic construction that things like Jane Austen had.

'It's a very early novel – the English novel was just getting started. They didn't know how to do novels then and Defoe tried to make his like journalism as much as possible. He thought novels shouldn't be like works of art – they should be authentic memoirs. *Robinson Crusoe* and *Moll Flanders* are both in the first person, like *Gulliver's Travels*, trying to make the reader believe they are a real account.

'I took the book to France on holiday and thought, "I don't really want to do this. I'm not sure how I'm going to do it." I remember my wife and I had a horrendous day driving down through traffic and our car practically gave up the ghost and we couldn't get anyone to mend it. We had one of those "crises abroad" days where there were desperate attempts to have rows in French and get someone to do something.

Writer Andrew Davies knew *Moll Flanders* from teaching it as a lecturer at Warwick University but remembered it as 'a pretty funny, ramshackle sort of book' and was reluctant to adapt it until he worked out that Moll telling her own story and talking to the camera was the way he would do it.

'In the end, we got ourselves a hotel room in this town where we had broken down. We still had half a bottle of duty-free whisky. We drank that and found a nice restaurant and then, suddenly, we relaxed, had a great big meal and lots to drink. I then thought, "I know how to do *Moll Flanders*! She's got to tell her own story and she's got to confront the audience a lot. She's saying, "'Suppose you were in this situation. What would you do?'" She would stop in the middle of robbing a child, turn to the camera and say, '"What am I going to do now?"' So I had a kind of idea of how to do it.

'When I got back home, I thought, "I'm still not quite sure about this." So I arranged a meeting with Gub Neal and Catriona McKenzie, and sort of talked myself into it and got very enthusiastic. They were both enthusiastic and liked the general approach I was taking to it.'

Gub recalls, 'At the meeting, we plied Andrew with enough wine to persuade him that actually doing an adaptation would be achievable, with sufficient time, and he was insistent about having four hours of screen time to do it in.'

The book has so many incidents in it that Andrew realised it would be necessary to choose the most important to include and felt there would be enough material to make four good episodes, each different from the others.

'We agreed on that,' he recalls. 'That stage was very plain-sailing compared with a lot of things I had been involved with, I think because we all saw eye to eye on it and Sally Head was very supportive. So I went away and wrote a pilot episode – the first episode – and everybody liked it. When the ITV Network Centre approved it, I went ahead and wrote the other three episodes.'

The first draft of Episode 1 was written in October 1994, but it was Christmas before Andrew and Granada received the go-ahead for the serial. During the spring of 1995, Andrew established a routine of scripting one episode every three weeks and even wrote part of Episode 2 during a week's tennis holiday in Spain.

Establishing authenticity in his scripts was a problem that did not concern Andrew too much because Defoe himself was vague about dates and times, and many of the characters – including several of Moll's husbands – were not even given names. This meant that Andrew had to make them up.

'He was writing in the eighteenth century, looking back to the relatively recent past,' says Defoe's twentieth-century adapter. 'I didn't think about it very much. I got some research done on conditions in Newgate and what it was like in Virginia. Apart from that, as far as the period went, I was just following the book.

'I did think the Restoration era was very jolly and hadn't really been done much on screen, so I thought for Moll's London days it would be nice to have that very free and easy period when Puritanism went out of the window and all the theatres reopened and there was a tremendous lot of mixing between the classes, particularly sexual mixing.

'You get all these actresses and prostitutes and semi-prostitutes, and there were beggars on the streets. I was trying in a way to find parallels between that century and this. It was very much to do with the rise of capitalism and the merchant classes, and the general expectation that if you wanted to get on you had to look out for yourself.

'Moll is very often faced with a choice, such as, "I don't want to swindle or rob this person. I don't really want to be a whore. But, if the alternative is starving, what would you do?" That's basically her attitude. Moll is a very reliant, enterprising character. She finds herself in situations like young homeless people do today. When they find themselves in desperate situations, they are likely to resort to crime.'

Writing from a woman's point of view was something that appealed to Andrew, too. 'It's something I always love to do,' he says. 'Perhaps it's some kind of perverse kink in my nature. I find it really fascinating – it's fascinated me since I was a kid. It's very interesting to try to work out what

OPPOSITE: The love of Moll's life is Jemmy (Daniel Craig), who tells her of his estate in Ireland, but he turns out to be down on his luck and makes his living as a highwayman.

women are feeling. Moll has what are usually thought of as masculine qualities — she's fearless, as well as cunning, sticks up for herself, is very bold and has a bad temper — but she's also capable of great tenderness.

'She certainly has very healthy appetites. She gets married five times, most of them bigamously, and she has other lovers. I wanted to reflect her prodigious sexual experience. Her first long affair is a very touching one. There she is, a very pretty semi-servant girl in this house, and the handsome elder son falls in love with her. It's halfway between that and a seduction, but she's as keen as he is. I haven't seen on screen a lot of that "how it is when you first get started in love and you're barmy about each other and you're at it all the time". That's something that's true to life.'

Andrew decided that the opening of each episode needed a device to take people into the story. Originally, he had the idea of starting in an eighteenth-century fairground, complete with jugglers, flame-eaters and various grotesques, and ending up at a sideshow of 'The Wickedest Woman in the World', with someone dressed up as Moll telling her tale.

When David Lascelles became producer, he believed the general idea was right but wanted to start each episode inside Newgate Prison with a gaoler acting as a master of ceremonies, showing well-to-do men and women around and building up to 'The Wickedest Woman in the World'. It was a fashionable entertainment of the time to see madmen, freaks and whores.

Something that was to cause a storm in the press was Andrew's decision to create the character of Lucy Diver as a composite of various thieves and pickpockets whom Moll teamed up with on the streets of London when she was struggling to make ends meet — and he hinted at a lesbian relationship between Moll and Lucy.

'I just thought I'd like to have it in,' he explains. 'I invented it. In the book, it's a period of Moll's life when she doesn't have any lover — she hasn't seen Jemmy for ages. The difficulty of dramatising that section of the book is that you get about 120 descriptions of small crimes that Moll committed and she has a number of partners who then just disappear. That would be pretty true to what the life of a criminal of that kind might be like, but it doesn't dramatise very well because you don't get to know any characters.

'So I teamed Moll up with another woman thief, who teaches her a lot, and thought, "Let's make Lucy someone who has got tired of men and prefers women". It's taking a liberty that I'm sure Defoe wouldn't mind, and there's nothing graphic in it — we don't learn what women do when they make love with one another.'

The sweeping nature of the novel, moving swiftly on from one incident to another — particularly in the second half — enabled Andrew to embellish some of the issues raised. For example, Defoe mentions that Moll's fourth husband, Jemmy, and his family are Catholics. 'But he never follows that up,' says Andrew. 'I thought that was quite something in those days, when Catholics were still persecuted. Then I wondered what happened if someone converts to Catholicism and found out that one of the things they have to do is to make a life confession. This presents Moll with a bit of a problem, of course! That never appears in the book.'

Deciding on how to end the story was the subject of much discussion. Andrew favoured dropping the low-key ending found in the book, where Moll doesn't get as far as the gallows. 'She manages to argue herself out of it,' says Andrew, 'and the evidence against Jemmy, who was awaiting trial in Newgate at the same time, was not tremendously strong. If he put in for transportation, he would get it. Once she escaped the gallows, we wanted to wind it up pretty quickly.'

As a result, the screen version shows Jemmy arriving in the nick of

Down on her luck, Moll teams up with 'the sharpest dip in England', Lucy Diver (Nicola Walker), a character created by Andrew Davies as a composite of the thieves Moll worked with in Daniel Defoe's book, with a hint of a lesbian relationship thrown in.

time with a pardon for Moll as she stands on the gallows, about to be hanged, and the two of them set sail for Virginia. The final part of the story, set in America, is much longer in the book.

'We used a bit of licence at times,' admits Andrew. 'Our excuse is that Shakespeare had anachronisms, so why shouldn't we? In one case, there was a song whose words fitted very well with the story, although in reality it was written later, but we decided to keep it. What was slightly unusual was that people said, "Bugger it! We like it. Let's go on and do it."

'I felt able to take far more freedoms with *Moll Flanders* because, although it's a terrific book and a great novel in some senses, it doesn't have a gang of admirers hanging on every word and not wanting the slightest thing changed. I think everyone who has read it regards it as a rather rough-and-ready sort of book with good and bad bits. To dramatise it, we've had to be quite bold with it and not be afraid of inventing things.

'I hope the programme makes a very big impact and that people will say, "This is not a BBC classic serial." I hope it will draw not only the audience that are interested in costume dramas and adaptations, but people who like to watch something that's a fast-moving story with a lot of sex and violence and humour in it — some of the younger male audience, which is notoriously the one you don't get at.'

Although he has written many original scripts for television, in recent years Andrew has become known for his adaptations of classics, and followed his script for *Moll Flanders* with others for *Emma* and *Jane Eyre*. 'I find it easier with adaptations,' he says, 'because I'm absolved of the problem of thinking up a good plot. That's something I find very difficult. I'm just delighted to have that work done for me, but I do think it's about time I got back to writing some of my own things. I really love doing adaptations, though — it's a different way of doing the books, really. And the "King of Adaptations" isn't a bad label to have.'

Meeting and marrying Jemmy means conversion to Catholicism for Moll, something not explored in Defoe's novel but used by Andrew Davies to embellish that part of the story.

CHAPTER TWO

BRINGING MOLL TO THE SCREEN

AVID LASCELLES, a freelance film and television producer who also happens to be a viscount, was finishing work as line producer on Ian McKellen's cinema version of *Richard III* when he visited Granada's newly appointed controller of drama, Gub Neal, in the summer of 1995 to discuss possible projects to work on. David had previously produced two series of *Inspector Morse*, as well as the TV movie *Wide Eyed and Legless* and the pilot *Paparazzo*, starring Nick Berry. Now he was interested to hear of Granada's intention to make *Moll Flanders*.

Taken on as producer, one of David's first jobs was to look at Andrew Davies's scripts, and he was instrumental in modifying the device that the adapter had used to ease viewers into each episode, switching from an eighteenth-century fairground with a *Moll Flanders* sideshow, followed by Moll telling her own story, direct to Newgate Prison, where a gaoler showed people round and ended up at Moll's cell, where she was waiting to go to the gallows.

'I thought the original idea was too confusing,' says David. 'I liked the theatrical device, but each episode had too many beginnings. I had the idea of combining those two things and using something that did happen in the seventeenth century, that fashionable folk would be taken on tours of Bedlam, the lunatic asylum, and Newgate Prison, by a corrupt gaoler. It's a bit of a freak show, and Andrew was being particularly mischievous and playful with the television audience, saying, "You're like this as well. You have switched on because you think this is going to be quite raunchy, with a bit of tit and bum." And that is true – there's an element of prurience about it.'

The original script editor, Catriona McKenzie, worked closely with Andrew, before becoming head of development in Granada's drama department and handing over to Susie Conklin, who came to the company from the BBC in 1995, after working as script editor on Andrew's adaptations of *Middlemarch* and *Pride and Prejudice*.

'I became involved before Andrew did his third and final draft,' says

Moll watches as Lucy Diver is caught red-handed with a jewelled watch she has stolen during scenes that director David Attwood admits were influenced by the Western film *The Wild Bunch*.

OPPOSITE: Some of the people whom Moll meets in the story, such as Mr Bland (James Fleet), had to be characterised quickly by Andrew Davies because their appearances are only short.

Susie, 'and tried to cast a new eye over it and look at a few places where I thought bits of the story didn't quite make sense. For instance, in Episode 4 there were eight or nine scenes of Moll thieving, but there's only so much you can do to demonstrate that period where the original book is packed with incident. We ended up taking some of the thieving scenes out.

'In the book, you don't stay with many characters that Moll meets along the way for very long, but for television you have to characterise them in some way very quickly. Rowland and Jemmy are fine in that they both have a good bit of story, but husbands like Dawkins and Mr Bland and, to a lesser extent, Lemuel are difficult because you don't have that much time to build up the relationship.

'That's why Andrew tried to find big, bold things like the Dawkins party sequence, which almost has a surreal quality to it, and the character himself is larger than life. You have to get an impression of a man who's going to spend money and have a laugh and a great time. Moll is attracted to that after her dreary marriage to Robin.'

With the script written, Granada Television production designer Stephen Fineren was already at work hunting for suitable filming locations and plan-

ning the sets. (See Chapter 4 for details.) He was adamant that the story should be firmly set in the seventeenth century before the Great Fire of London, when England was still a stone and half-timbered place architecturally. 'It's different from what we're used to seeing,' says David Lascelles, 'with dirty, off-white colours. There isn't a lot of it still around, so that presented particular problems.

'What we were planning was four hours of television, a very episodic story with Moll constantly on the move. It has a restless spirit and we had to represent that range of places in the story, and you have to find a way of doing that compactly and economically. You either have to find something that's written in the script or build it or rewrite it. We have done a certain amount of all three.

'To find it, you have to go to where it is. There isn't much seventeenth-century stuff in the North of England, where Granada is based. So we ended up filming in Shropshire, Warwickshire, Derbyshire, Wiltshire, Cornwall and Lincolnshire. We had to find a balance between what we could build and where we had to go to film. I had always felt certain that we would have to build a set for the streets of London because we wouldn't find anything authentic anywhere. It also became clear that we would have to build the Newgate Prison interiors — there aren't many medieval prisons around.'

The next stage in the production was to hire a director. David was emphatic that it would not be one who had experience of period drama because he wanted someone 'without any baggage'. So, in late 1995, he spoke to eight different directors, gauging whether his vision tied in with theirs.

Eventually, David Attwood was taken on. He had experience of making police series such as *Rockliffe's Babies* and *The Bill*, as well as the Alan Plater-created *Tales from Sherwood Forest* and a Channel Four–British Screen film, *Wild West*, a comedy following an Asian youngster's dream of becoming a country and western singer. He also directed the BBC's 1995 Screen Two drama *Saigon Baby*, starring Kerry Fox and Douglas Hodge as a couple based in Thailand who want to adopt a child and become embroiled in a baby-trafficking business run by John Hurt in Vietnam.

'I was very struck immediately by David's enthusiasm and the freshness of his approach,' says David Lascelles. 'We talked a lot about how we could make a period film in a modern way, in the same way that, of its time, something like the film *Tom Jones* did very well in the sixties. What was fresh about that then was making a period film in a *nouvelle vague* kind of way.'

David Attwood felt his own experience on *The Bill* was useful in terms of the pace and editing for *Moll Flanders*. 'What's great about *The Bill*,' he says, 'is that you have to tell a story in twenty-two minutes and you don't have any great photography. The acting and the story are all that count, and there are good directors who couldn't direct *The Bill*.

'*Moll Flanders* should glance off the screen and be irreverent, totally like Defoe. I could see different influences coming to bear on different parts of the story. The extravagance of Ken Russell is my influence for the flamboyant section featuring Moll's second husband, Dawkins, and Sam Peckinpah's Western *The Wild Bunch* came to mind for the relationship between Moll and Lucy Diver and all their stealing.

'The challenge for a director is getting the tone and balance right. I've seen theatre productions of *Moll Flanders*, where they do the picaresque romp but don't engage with Moll as a character. But, then, if you decide to create a real world and make the audience sympathise with her predicament, you can end up making a very serious drama, which the book

isn't either. You have to warm to the character but, at the same time, say to the audience, "This is not your average period drama." I had an interest in the story and the period, mainly the fact that it wasn't the nineteenth century but the seventeenth century. The last good film of that period was *Tom Jones* in the sixties and it has never been repeated.'

David liked the modified device of entering into each episode through the gaoler showing people round Newgate, combined with Moll talking to the camera. 'You engage the audience with Moll,' he says,

Producer David Lascelles (left) discusses a shot with director David Attwood during location filming for Granada Television's production of *Moll Flanders*.

'by going from the freak-show element to Moll talking to the audience. To start with, you can think, "I'm a member of this rabble coming to see a freak show," then as a television viewer you are invited into a personal relationship with Moll. You then become a friend whom Moll confides in and, at moments in her life when she's not happy, a friend she rejects. There is also the device of Moll's voiceover, which is totally about telling the story, recollected in tranquillity from Virginia years later.'

The production was already pre-sold to America as part of a package of Granada programmes bought by WGBH of Boston, but casting the central role of Moll proved to be particularly difficult, despite the number of well-known actresses who were auditioned for the part.

In all, almost forty actresses were auditioned. 'We didn't want anyone to bring the wrong sort of period baggage with them,' says David Lascelles, 'so we ruled out any of those actresses who had starred in the recent big adaptations on television. That wouldn't have been doing us or them a favour.

'We had to see just about every beautiful actress in England aged twenty to thirty. David Attwood and I saw them all with our casting directors, Gail Stevens and Andy Prior. It's such a huge, huge part, appearing in virtually every scene during four hours of television, ageing twenty years in the process, going through the darkest tragedy to the bawdiest comedy and never allowing herself to become a victim. Not many English actresses have that kind of wild spirit. There are French actresses who have that innocent but knowing kind of animal quality. Brigitte Bardot in her heyday had it.

'Our first choice was Minnie Driver, who starred in *Mr Wroe's Virgins* and *The Politician's Wife*. She does have those qualities, but she wasn't available – she was working in America. We then went through a whole long list of actresses, including Emily Lloyd, Helen Baxendale of *Cardiac Arrest*, Helen McCrory – who's best known as a stage actress – Beatie Edney, Samantha Morton and Lena Headey from *Band of Gold*, and Angeline Ball.

'These are all really good actresses in their different ways. You can see some of them playing different aspects of Moll. You can see Samantha and Lena playing the young Moll, but I couldn't ever believe them as an embittered thirty-six-year-old waiting to go to the scaffold. We couldn't really see some of those actresses playing the younger, more innocent Moll. Emily Lloyd has a cheekiness about her that's good, but we weren't convinced that anything she said or anything we had seen her in would allow her to play the darker sides of the story.

'We watched videos, met actresses, talked about the script and read scenes with them. We had our short list, but no one felt convinced that any of them could have done the whole range of what was required. So we cast our net wider. I knew Alex Kingston, having seen her in one film and on television a bit, and I knew her a bit socially. The casting directors also knew her.

'We gave each actress three scenes to see how they could play a range of emotions. The first was Moll the virgin in a seduction scene with Rowland, the Mayor's son, in Episode 1. The second was Moll as the consummate seductress with Mr Bland in the scene where he stays on guard in her bedroom but ends up in her bed, she playing with a man like a fisherman with his trout. And the last was Moll stealing the necklace from a little girl and dreaming that she nearly throttles her. Alex gave a dynamite reading and showed similar qualities to Minnie Driver.

Alex Kingston was cast in the role of Moll only after many well-known actresses were auditioned and rejected.

Being seduced by Rowland (Colin Buchanan) was one of the scenes that Alex Kingston ran through by herself during a read-through that producer David Lascelles described as 'dynamite'.

'So, at that stage, Alex became a very, very serious contender indeed. Then it was a question of using our own instincts that one particular actress was going to be good in the role rather than someone else. Alex has a lot of experience but not a high profile. You then go through a process of trying to talk yourself out of it. You test the thesis as harshly as you can, but we convinced ourselves and convinced Gub Neal that she was right. The further it has gone on, the more right I think we were. It was a gamble that paid off.'

For Alex, taking on the role of Moll posed problems – she was committed to star in a stage play, Ibsen's *The Lady from the Sea*, at the Bridwell Theatre, a London fringe venue. 'The first I heard of *Moll Flanders* was when my agent, Lou Coulson, phoned me in rehearsals for the play,' recalls Alex. 'She asked if I could go across to see David Lascelles and David Attwood at the LWT studios. I told her I couldn't because I was in the middle of rehearsals. Then, my agent rang back later and said the two Davids were prepared to wait until 6.30p.m., when I finished, so I went.

'But I was in the mode for playing the lead in *The Lady from the Sea*, whereas when you go to interviews you usually try to interpret the character you're hoping to play through the clothes you wear, for instance. I went along not really caring because I was so involved in the play. I just chatted to the two Davids, they gave me the scripts and asked me to go away and prepare three scenes to read the following day.

'When I went home, I thought I couldn't just read those three scenes

out of context, so I decided to read all four episodes and couldn't put it down! In the morning, I woke up and carried on reading. By the time I went back to see David Attwood, who was with the casting directors, Gail Stevens and Andy Prior, I had read the whole script but not really prepared the three scenes. Nevertheless, David was very complimentary and I left with the two casting directors saying they thought that David was very interested in me.

'But a week after going for the interview, I heard that Gub Neal and Andrew Davies wanted to meet this person that the two Davids were keen on. I wasn't nervous at all. I was still involved very heavily in the stage play of *The Lady from the Sea*, so that's where all my energies lay. They sent a car for me at the theatre during my lunch break, I chatted with them and they didn't ask me to read again. It was just a nice, friendly chat, talking to Gub and Andrew about how I saw Moll and interpreted Andrew's creation.

'That was on a Friday and, on the following Monday, my agent rang to tell me the news that I'd got the part. She just burst into tears on the telephone. What was so great was that the producer and director were

The scene in which Moll dreams about almost strangling a little girl (Jenna Hodges) was one that Alex Kingston had to read for her audition.

Ivan Strasburg was brought in as director of photography after work on documentaries and drama, including *Agatha Christie's Poirot* and *Cracker*, for which he won a BAFTA award.

prepared to take a risk with someone who wasn't a household name. That happens so rarely nowadays in television.'

Arrangements had to be made for Alex to leave the stage production of *The Lady from the Sea* a week before it was due to close and there was little time to cast the other characters in *Moll Flanders* because finding the right actress to take the lead role had taken taken seven weeks. It also gave the costume designer, Trisha Biggar, only four weeks to work on Alex's dresses.

'Although we held back on casting anyone until we had cast Moll, we *were* seeing people,' recalls David Lascelles. 'The casting directors knew Daniel Craig, having worked on *Our Friends in the North*, and were very enthusiastic about putting him in the role of Jemmy. "Everybody's going to be wanting him after that," they were saying.

'We went casting crazy with all these people we had been seeing over the previous two months and cast nearly the whole production in one afternoon. But by the time of the read-through, just a week before we started filming, we still hadn't cast two of Moll's husbands.'

The two Davids had clear views on how the drama should look. 'Alex plays from eighteen to thirty-six,' says David Lascelles, 'so we wanted it to look like her life was quite an epic period and went through quite major changes. The obvious way to do that was with costumes.

'You end up having to rationalise things to create a design look, and our production designer, Stephen Fineren, was very keen to set it in a very different era from the one you normally see British costume dramas in – usually Regency into Georgian. In a way we were making life difficult for ourselves, but it was done to distinguish the look from anything else.'

Putting a film crew together was relatively easy because most were Granada staff, but several freelances were hired in key creative positions. As well as director David Attwood and costume designer Trisha Biggar, there was director of photography Ivan Strasburg, who has split his career between drama and documentaries, having worked with such acclaimed directors as Ken Loach, Peter Hall, Alan Clarke, Chris Menges and Philip Saville.

'We were doing a big period drama, which David Attwood and I had not done before and Granada had not done for a while,' says David Lascelles, 'so you either go for someone who has a proven track record in doing this kind of work or go for people you know are good. I'd worked with Ivan on *Paparazzo* and David Attwood was keen to work with him as well. Trisha Biggar, the costume designer, had worked with David on *Wild West* and *Saigon Baby*.'

With the problems of late casting and, consequently, little time to prepare costumes, filming was put back several days. The ten-week shoot began in March 1996, ran through to May, and the four-hour serial had to be ready for screening in September, although the transmission dates were eventually changed to December. 'We had a tight deadline,' says David Lascelles. 'The way the ITV commissioning system works these days is that the broadcaster doesn't get its money from the network until the production is transmitted. So all broadcasters are trying to make everything as late as possible. It was necessary for us to increase the pre-production period by almost a week at the expense of editing time because I felt we needed more time to get it ready.'

CHAPTER THREE

THE CAST

Moll Flanders
Alex Kingston

LANDING THE ROLE of Moll Flanders was a dream come true for virtual unknown Alex Kingston, but the actress had no nerves or embarrassment when it came to performing sex scenes in the four-hour production. 'I have sex on screen seventeen times,' she says, with a touch of humorous glee. 'I've done a lot of modelling for artists ever since I was a young girl, and being naked doesn't worry me if I'm modelling for them because they are looking at the body as a form to interpret.

'If I were doing a television drama or a movie in which the sex scenes were gratuitous or had a titillating veil, that would intimidate me because I would be incredibly conscious of my body. But because Moll is so earthy, the sex scenes are so real. I don't care if people see my lumps and bumps. None of it is gratuitous – it's all rather refreshing.'

Alex even entered into the spirit of the time, when women wore no knickers, and discarded her own during filming. 'Because they didn't wear them in the seventeenth century, none were designed for me,' says Alex. 'I gave Christopher Fulford, who plays my second husband, Dawkins, a real eyeful when during the draper's party scene I hitched my skirt up and flashed at him. He was *so* shocked!'

Alex came to the production, with a gruelling, ten-week filming schedule in which her character would be seen in almost every scene, straight from a fringe theatre stage play, *The Lady from the Sea*, in which she had been starring for four weeks before handing over to another actress so that she could take on the role of Moll.

'The actress who took over was already in the play,' says Alex, 'but I couldn't help her because I was going to costume fittings for *Moll* at 9a.m. every day, and would stay there till 4p.m., go straight to the theatre, do the play, go home, sleep and wake up again the following morning to go straight back for costume fittings. I was completely exhausted because *The Lady from the Sea* was such a huge role. We started

Alex Kingston, enjoying a chat between takes with Daniel Craig while filming *Moll Flanders*, started work on the production immediately after starring in *The Lady from the Sea* at a London fringe theatre.

filming on *Moll* the day after I finished in the play.'

All this meant that thirty-three-year-old Alex had little time to research the part of Moll. 'If I'd had time,' she says, 'I would have bought lots of books, but I didn't. However, I have done quite a few classical plays, and when I was doing *The Country Wife*, I read a book called *The Weaker Vessel*, by Antonia Fraser, which was about women's lot in the seventeenth century, so I took that with me when we started filming.

'Before I read the book, I even thought that Moll was some sort of whore or highwaywoman. But she has a moral stance. She knows that money rules the world and she needs money and will do anything to marry into money. But she certainly won't sleep with a man unless he promises her marriage.

'The one scene that really made me interested in the character was the dream scene where Moll almost strangles a little girl. What I loved about it was that she is the heroine of the piece and she's someone whom you like but, at the same time, you don't like the fact that you like her because she's fallible. I immediately thought of Myra Hindley and the fact that a woman who has had children can, for a fleeting moment, contemplate killing a child just for a necklace.

'But it wasn't a struggle for me to understand Moll as a woman. She is the most wonderful life spirit and, if someone has that, it doesn't matter what age they live in. I think one thing that women watching today will find quite interesting is her attitude to children. The only thing that gives away the fact that *Moll Flanders* was written by a man, as opposed to a woman, is that Defoe doesn't dwell on her pregnancies or childbearing. There's a wonderful line where Moll talks to camera and says, "Well, I'm not as motherly as some women. We aren't made all the same way." There are many women now who don't want children because they want their careers.

Alex herself was getting over the break-up of her marriage to actor Ralph Fiennes when she started filming *Moll Flanders*. 'Acting on stage in *The Lady from the Sea* had already been a sort of therapy for me when that happened,' she says. 'In a funny way, being given a part like that and what the character was going through in terms of having a stable relationship with a very loving husband and having this desire to live and feeling trapped and wanting to find or experience the darker side of herself through the stranger, I could relate it more to my husband and understand his need for freedom or exploration or whatever.

'What was lovely about being given the chance then to do *Moll* was that I just rediscovered myself. I had been through a very bad period in my life and, like Moll, I thought I couldn't survive. But I found I was able to pick myself up and start again. I had been through something so traumatic, but I'm still here and people believed in me and wanted me for me, as opposed to wanting me because I was associated with Ralph Fiennes. It was the most fantastically timely confidence-booster. I feel very much that I'm earthed again and I'm looking forward to the future.'

One happy surprise for Alex during the week-long rehearsals for *Moll Flanders* was the arrival of her sister, who had just left drama school. But the star was shocked to find out that Nicola Kingston was playing baby Moll's mother in the opening scenes of the serial.

'We were rehearsing in Soho and just coming up to a lunch break,' recalls Alex. 'I thought, "What the hell is she doing here?" She said, "I'm auditioning to play your mother." Afterwards, she came up to me and told me she'd got the part.

'It works very well because we don't look very similar but we have the same deep voice. Although Nicola doesn't look anything like Diana Rigg did in real life when she was young, you can believe she is the younger version of Diana as she is seen in *Moll Flanders*.'

Alex herself trained at RADA, but she already had acting experience as a child through attending a drama school from the age of thirteen. Two years later, her teacher decided to become an agent and Alex soon found herself appearing in two of the most notorious girls' schools in screen history – Grange Hill and St Trinian's.

First, she auditioned for *Grange Hill*, the children's drama serial set in a London comprehensive school. 'All of us who attended our teacher's drama classes were put up for the part of a judo bully,' Alex recalls, 'and I said I'd never done any judo in my life. She said, "It doesn't matter –

just tell them you're a black belt and it will be fine." So I went along for the interview and they asked if I had done any judo before. I said yes but couldn't bring myself to say I was a black belt, so I said I was an orange belt, not even knowing if there was such a thing, and they gave me the part.

'I immediately started going to a judo club at night after school and attained an orange belt, which did actually exist. Then I acted this character called Jill Harcourt in *Grange Hill* for four or five episodes.'

Shortly afterwards, Alex appeared in the feature film *The Wildcats of St Trinian's*, which was an attempt to recreate the St Trinian's films of old. 'As a child, I loved those films,' says Alex. 'I always wanted to be one of those girls with hockey sticks and hair sticking through a straw hat! So I was thrilled when I got a part as a sixth former. I was put in black stockings and a little skirt, and had to sit sexily on desks and motorbikes with all these other sixth formers who were played by Page 3 girls. Unfortunately, it was a terrible movie, not anything like the old St Trinian's films.'

One of Alex's greatest learning experiences came after graduating from RADA, when she was cast by director Peter Greenaway as Adele, the cook's niece who looked after the restaurant accounts, in his film *The Cook The Thief His Wife & Her Lover*, starring Helen Mirren, Michael Gambon, Richard Bohringer and Alan Howard. Two scenes in which she had dialogue were eventually cut from the filming schedule, but she was seen in the film as a single waitress among many waiters.

'I ended up standing around the set most of the time,' says Alex, 'and it was really fascinating because I was able to watch the different styles of these four heavyweight players. Michael Gambon's performance was so theatrical. Richard Bohringer was continually frustrated because he couldn't speak any English and he didn't always know what he was required to do. Alan Howard was a lovely man but quite quiet and introverted.

'Then there was Helen Mirren. I would watch her day in and day out. She was doing nothing! I got really worried. I thought, "It's going to be a disaster. She's not doing anything." But when I saw the film on screen, I thought, "My God!" She did seemingly so little that you couldn't notice it standing next to her, but the camera picked up everything. Her performance is just extraordinary. It was a real education to me. I wasn't long out of drama school and it was wonderful for me to see someone underplaying to perfection.'

Since then, Alex has appeared in several films, including *Carrington*, in the role of Frances Partridge, and various television programmes. She has been in *The Bill* four times and had parts in series such as *A Killing on the Exchange*, *Hannay* and *Soldier Soldier* before playing a lawyer in the Jimmy Nail series *Crocodile Shoes*. Paul Knight, the producer, subsequently cast her as Katherine Roberts, the tough new customs officer, in the second series of *The Knock*, which was screened while she was making *Moll Flanders*. 'I liked the part of Katherine and had fun playing her,' says the actress. 'It was six months' work and very good experience.'

On stage, Alex has long experience of playing the classics, including five productions with the Royal Shakespeare Company. 'In *Moll Flanders*, Andrew Davies's writing is a mix between contemporary and classical,' she says. 'I find the language really easy, perhaps because of my background.

'I'd still love to play Lady Macbeth on stage, or Rosalind in *As You Like It*. I've been to Hollywood as somebody else's other half, but it really doesn't appeal to me. What I couldn't bear is the fascism of beauty and I would become incredibly self-conscious and intimidated. I just wouldn't want to be ruled by people whose attitude is so superficial. I'd much prefer to be involved in European filming.'

Jemmy
Daniel Craig

PLAYING GEORDIE PEACOCK in *Our Friends in the North* turned Daniel Craig into a heart-throb, and filming on more than a hundred locations for months on end in the biggest drama serial ever commissioned by BBC2 prepared him well for his role as Moll Flanders's special love, Jemmy.

Our Friends in the North, Peter Flannery's story following the lives of

four Geordie friends through three decades, saw Daniel's character leave Tyneside for London, become involved in a Soho porn empire, suffer a drink problem, deal in drugs and get thrown into gaol.

The final episode of the nine-part saga was screened in March 1996, just a week before filming on *Moll Flanders* began, and by then *Our Friends in the North* had become BBC2's most popular programme, with more than five million viewers. It meant that, as with Alex Kingston, Granada Television had a previously unknown actor becoming a star shortly before being seen by viewers in its new production.

'I met the producer and director after Christmas,' recalls Daniel. 'At that stage, Moll had still not been cast, but they were certainly looking at me for the part of Jemmy. We discussed the role and the whole feel of the piece. It's fairly straightforward. Jemmy's a highwayman out for what he can get but, hopefully, he has an awful lot of charm. Despite the fact that he messes about so much, he is a good bloke.'

Jemmy is first seen briefly when Moll arrives in London after the death of her first husband, Robin. On horseback, he holds her gaze for a few seconds and tips his hat to her as she passes in her carriage.

He is not seen again until Moll has left her third husband in Virginia and returns to England, travelling to Lancaster and passing herself off as the wealthy Lady Flanders. At a society ball, she is swept off her feet by Jemmy, who boasts of an estate in Ireland but is more often to be found on the road as a highwayman. His proposal soon follows and she agrees to convert to his Roman Catholic faith.

This time it is true love for Moll but, while staying at Westchester

Inn after their wedding, on the way to Jemmy's estate in Ireland, he admits that he has no money and she does likewise. By the morning, he is gone, having stolen a horse from the inn stables and left a note saying he is taking to the road again to get money.

Moll's subsequent stagecoach trip to London is halted by Jemmy and his cohorts stopping the vehicle and ordering the occupants out to hand over their money and jewels. Taking Moll to one side, Jemmy gives her some of the valuables. The next time she sees him is when he is arrested and taken to Newgate Prison, where she herself awaits the gallows.

Apart from Alex Kingston, Daniel was the only actor to be involved in the whole of the filming. Scenes of his were filmed regularly throughout the three-month shooting schedule, although he is seen mostly in the third and fourth episodes. This meant that he was not needed on occasional days and on others he would hang around waiting to be called.

'I'm the only other one who goes the whole way through, but my workload is less than half of Alex's,' he says. 'Actually, it's often less of a struggle to be on every day. It hasn't been hard for me, but I prefer being on all the time.'

Although costume drama was not totally new to Daniel — who appeared alongside Sean Bean in *Sharpe's Eagle*, playing a soldier who tried to rape a Spanish countess and shot Sharpe in the leg, before being killed — *Moll Flanders* marked a new departure for him.

'It's very different from anything else I've done,' he says. 'We've got horses, big costumes, fabulous locations and there's a lot to do. It isn't just a question of turning up and shooting a scene. You have a lot of extras and have to make every scene look right before filming starts, moving horses and carriages into position, for example, which means there's more waiting around than usual.

'But I've had a ball. We've been all over the country and had a look at some wonderful locations. The piece has a real pace to it that drives the whole thing along. You can never tell exactly how something's going to turn out, but you can get an idea of the feel of it from the people you're working with. Everybody has been into it and known what they've been doing.'

Before *Moll Flanders* and *Our Friends in the North*, Daniel appeared on television in *The Young Indiana Jones Chronicles*, playing a Prussian captain in the German army, and had guest roles in *Heartbeat*, *Drop the Dead Donkey* and *Between the Lines*. He also acted in two films, *The Kid in King Arthur's Court* and the apartheid drama *The Power of One*.

'I'm not really interested in looking for the best roles,' he says. 'I've done a lot of bits and pieces on television. A lot of it has been to pay the rent. I'm more interested in looking for pieces I find interesting.'

Daniel's stage work included a year with the National Theatre performing in *Angels in America*. 'Then *Our Friends in the North* came up, which was ground-breaking,' he recalls. '*Moll Flanders* came afterwards. I don't want to do stock things and felt this had a different feel to it. If I have a choice I will make the choice.

'I go through life thinking it's all going to end tomorrow. I'd like to do classical theatre, but it would have to be the right sort of thing. But I don't think I'd want to do a classical piece for a long run because they are so exhausting. In the theatre, you have to regenerate every night.

'Alex has done a lot more classical theatre than I have and it's been great working with her. Her asset is that she is not a big name and, being given a part like this, she puts that much more effort into it. I was glad that they were not casting a name but a good actress because I thought this would be someone who was hungry to take on the role rather than someone just furthering their own career. She's been incredibly happy doing it and that should come through on screen. Alex's enthusiasm just shines.'

Rowland
Colin Buchanan

MOLL'S FIRST LOVE is Rowland, son of Mayor Richardson, and they conduct their steamy relationship behind the backs of the family. He promises to wed her when he comes to inherit his father's estate, for he would be cut off without a penny if he married out of his class before then.

But that will be years away, and in the meantime, the couple have to keep their love secret. Rowland's younger brother, Robin, declares his own love for Moll, unwittingly helping to cover up the affair. But it is a shock to her when Rowland suggests she accepts Robin's hand in marriage.

Although it leaves Moll heartbroken, it becomes clear that Rowland is determined that this should happen and, worried about losing them both and being thrown out on the streets, she accepts Robin's proposal – at the same time telling Rowland that she could not be 'the mistress of one man and the wife of his brother'. So she parts with her first love, marries Robin and later hears that Rowland has wed, too.

As Granada Television began filming *Moll Flanders*, actor Colin

Buchanan, who plays Rowland, was seen making it to the altar on television in his role as DS Peter Pascoe in the crime series *Dalziel and Pascoe*. The series teamed Colin with Warren Clarke as two Yorkshire CID officers, Warren an old-style copper who has come up through the ranks and Colin a whiz-kid university graduate with a social science degree.

This was a contrast to his previous TV success as happy-go-lucky Hodge in the Territorial Army comedy-drama *All Quiet on the Preston Front* and its sequel, *Preston Front*. Being the son of a former Marine and growing up in an Army family was a help to the actor during the first series, although his character packed in the Territorial Army when he returned in the sequel. Colin's other television appearances have included guest roles in *A Touch of Frost* and *London's Burning*.

Robin
Ian Driver

ROBIN, THE YOUNGER of Mr Richardson's sons, is Moll's first husband – but not her first lover. Little does he know that his older brother has already taken her virginity. Robin is so besotted with Moll that he declares his feelings to all around and, when Rowland tells Moll that he will lose his inheritance if he marries her, she eventually accepts Robin's proposal of marriage.

'He is completely infatuated with Moll and cannot understand why she is at first reluctant to marry him,' says Ian Driver, who plays Robin. 'He has no reason to believe his brother is seeing her. He rather idolises him.

'The whole humour of the part comes from the fact that Robin doesn't ever consider Moll's point of view. It drives him crazy when she originally refuses to marry him. He goes through all the reasons he can logically think of – that his parents and the people of Colchester won't approve – but he doesn't care.

'He sees in Moll an inner beauty and a good nature. He has grown up with her in the house and she can do everything that his real sisters cannot. She can really play the piano very well, although she's never been taught, and she sings like an angel.'

So Moll weds Robin, has two children and lives through a loveless marriage for five years, until Robin's sudden death. She then leaves their two children with his parents and sets off for London.

Actor Ian Driver took on the role of Robin after working for five years, on and off, with the Royal Shakespeare Company in productions such as *The Duchess of Malfi*, *Pericles*, *Two Gentlemen of Verona* and *The Tempest*. His other television parts have included Ned Plymdale in *Middlemarch* and policemen in both *A Touch of Frost* and *The Chief*. He also played the son of actor Martin Shaw in *The Greater Good*, a television drama about a married MP involved in a homosexual relationship.

In *Middlemarch*, in which his character fell in love with Rosamond Vincy – played by Trevyn McDowell, who acts Mrs Seagrave in *Moll Flanders* – he found himself in a similar situation to that in *Moll Flanders*. 'His love was thwarted,' explains Ian. 'But Ned was much more of a snob than Robin. He was *nouveau riche* and his mother was pushing him into this marriage. With Robin, it's a question of love. He is a young lad who becomes a man through the process of wooing.'

Daniel Dawkins
Christopher Fulford

AFTER ROBIN'S DEATH, Moll heads for London with a small fortune in her pocket and a desire to marry again. Daniel Dawkins, a draper who has come into his father's inheritance, wins her hand but that inheritance and Moll's own money is soon spent, the bailiffs arrive and Dawkins runs away to France, never to be seen again.

Christopher Fulford was clear about how he wanted to portray Dawkins. 'It's a huge character,' says the actor. 'He is a very flamboyant man who is genuinely just trying to have a good time with the money that his father couldn't enjoy. So he has bought into wealth and given himself a title, the Duke of Dawkinshire, and he blows all the money very quickly.

'Leaving Moll wasn't a question of being ungentlemanly. He has the money, has a good time, then clears off. I think she probably knows that all the time. There wasn't this sense of decency then. I've always thought when I've done Restoration plays on stage, such as *The Relapse*, that these people think in the moment – it isn't inward and introspective.'

Moll's marriage to Dawkins signals her first experience of London as an adult. This gave the actors and crew a chance to contrast her days in Colchester during the Puritan era.

'Initially,' says Christopher, 'we were going to play it very much in the period slightly before the Restoration. But when we talked about it, we thought it would be a nice excuse to use her first appearance in London after being in the country to be involved in the whole of the Restoration and the flamboyance of it – the costumes, parties and theatre.'

The actor's previous experience of costume drama on screen includes playing Napoleon in the television mini-series *Scarlet & Black*. He has also acted on stage with the Old Vic company in *Lancelot and Guinevere*, *The Merchant of Venice* and *Macbeth*.

Christopher, whose many television appearances include roles in *Made in Britain*, *The Ruth Rendell Mysteries*, *A Touch of Frost*, *Cracker*, *Prime Suspect* and the male lead, ex-policeman Hal Hawksley, in *The Sculptress*, found that the costume and make-up helped him to get into the role of Dawkins.

'As soon as I get the lipstick and the wig on, I become like some fop,' he says. 'In fact, I've based him on Danny La Rue. I think drag is very interesting – it's very funny, very sexy. The whole of this period we're representing is sexy and the women were all up for grabs. These people used to frolic around and have a good time without worrying about anything.'

Lemuel
Tom Ward

MOLL'S FORTUNES SEEM to take a turn for the better when she travels to Chatham and meets sea captain Lemuel, who soon convinces her that he is not looking for a wealthy wife, contrary to her assertion that seafaring men like their 'whores to be handsome and well shaped' but their wives to have money. Wedding bells are soon ringing again, even though Moll knows that her second husband is alive and well in France.

Lemuel takes Moll across the sea to live on the tobacco plantations owned by his mother in Virginia, and for years the couple live an idyllic existence there and she gives birth to three children, until Lemuel's mother tells Moll that she had been transported there and had her baby taken from her seven days after birth.

Realising the awful truth – that this woman is her mother, and Lemuel her own brother – Moll withdraws all conjugal rights but later decides that sleeping with Lemuel again and commiting incest is only what she had done before in innocence and ignorance. However, she later collapses in church and subsequently refuses to speak to Lemuel. When Moll reveals the reasons for her behaviour, Lemuel is horrified. Eventually, he agrees that she must return to England and he will keep the children and tell people that she has died so that he will be free to marry again.

Actor Tom Ward had made only a handful of television appearances before taking the role of Lemuel. He played Chamberlayne in *Pride and Prejudice*, as well as acting in the teenage series *Island* — about seven youngsters working on Jersey during the summer — and the wartime drama *No Bananas*.

While studying at Oxford University, the actor performed in classics such as *As You Like It*, *The Alchemist* and *Cymbeline*, took the title role in *Hamlet* at the Oxford Shakespeare Festival and played Huld in *The Trial*, a seventieth-anniversary production at the Oxford Playhouse. Trained as a stage fighter — hand-to-hand and with sword — Tom has fenced for Britain. Ironically, his own riding skills were not needed in *Moll Flanders*.

Mrs Golightly
Diana Rigg

ON MOLL AND Lemuel's arrival in Virginia, Lemuel's formidable mother, Mrs Golightly, is initially disappointed that her daughter-in-law has no fortune, but she quickly puts that aside and resolves that they should live as one big, happy family, and Moll obliges by bearing three children.

But the dream is shattered when Moll learns that Mrs Golightly is her mother and Lemuel her brother. Eventually, after making life hell for Lemuel, Moll reveals the truth to his mother, who is delighted to have found her daughter but agrees that Moll must return to England by herself.

Diana Rigg, who plays Moll's mother, is forever destined to be remembered on television as John Steed's karate-chopping sidekick Emma Peel in *The Avengers*, which is still repeated around the world, although she actually appeared in it for only two series.

Emma Peel, dressed in catsuits, hipster pants and thigh-length skirts, became an image of the sixties and the programme was at its height during her time in it, with a worldwide television audience of thirty million. Diana came to the role after working with the Royal Shakespeare

Company and returned to the stage after the 1967 series, as well as starring in the James Bond film *On Her Majesty's Secret Service*.

Her subsequent television appearances have included *In This House of Brede, King Lear, Bleak House* – as Lady Dedlock – the TV movie *A Hazard of Hearts* and *Mother Love*, the series written by Andrew Davies in which she portrayed the obsessive mother of a composer played by David McCallum, winning the actress a BAFTA award.

Her early roles with the Royal Shakespeare Company included Bianca in *The Taming of the Shrew*, Helena in *A Midsummer Night's Dream*, Adriana in *The Comedy of Errors*, Cordelia in *King Lear* and Viola in *Twelfth Night*. In the West End, she has played Héloïse in *Abelard and Héloïse*, Eliza Dolittle in *Pygmalion* and Ruth Carson in Tom Stoppard's *Night and Day*.

Of her sexuality, Diana once said, 'I cannot define it, I am not aware of it and I certainly don't peddle it. I cannot flirt. It makes me laugh.'

Clergyman
John Savident

PLAYING THE CLERGYMAN who shares Moll's stagecoach journey from Westchester Inn to London, following Jemmy's departure on their wedding night, provided John Savident with the chance to give a larger-than-life performance in *Moll Flanders*.

'I chatted with the director about this priest,' he says, 'and told him the idea I had for the character. He would have a particular way of speaking, rather like one or two MPs who pronounce their s's as a 'sh'. There was also an old actor called Robert Atkins who spoke like that.

'It gives a richness and fruitiness to the character, especially when he talks in the stagecoach about all the wickedness Moll might encounter in London, all the sexual acts like "fornication, sodomy, fellatio and cunnilingus, tribadism, unbridled concupiscence on every street corner". *Moll Flanders* is a satire anyway – it's fun.'

When their stagecoach is held up by Jemmy and all those inside are lined up to have their valuables taken, the clergyman is relieved of his body belt. 'He turns from this booming, bellowing gentleman who no doubt scares the pants off his congregation and then he faints,' says John.

The actor filmed his scenes during a three-week break from *Coronation Street*, having become a regular in the serial as master butcher Fred Elliot, renowned for his pies, wheeling and dealing and lack of subtlety.

Born in Guernsey, but brought up in Ashton-under-Lyne, Lancashire, John gave up a career in the police force after six years to turn to acting full time and, since making his television début in the sixties John Thaw series *Redcap*, has appeared in dozens of screen productions. On TV, he played George Askew, the Ashton family's solicitor, in *A Family at War* and, more recently, John Raffles in *Middlemarch*. His films include *A Clockwork Orange*, *Gandhi*, *The Remains of the Day* and *Othello*.

John also has extensive experience on stage, having acted in National Theatre productions such as *The Beggar's Opera*, *St Joan* and *Coriolanus*, and played other classical roles at the Old Vic and Chichester Festival Theatre. His West End productions include *The Phantom of the Opera*, playing Monsieur Firmin in the original cast – a part that still earns him royalties as a result of his performance on the multi-million-selling record.

'Actors do television most of the time for the money, then dash off to the theatre,' says John. 'But when something like *Moll Flanders* comes along, you read the script and want to go for it.'

Mr Bland
James Fleet

BANKER JOHN BLAND meets Moll on her stagecoach trip to London, when they and their fellow-travellers are held up by highwayman Jemmy. After the ordeal, Mr Bland offers to protect her that night, and she suggests that he sit in a chair with his two pistols, facing away from her bed towards the door.

But it is not long before she suggests he might be more comfortable lying on her covers, with his pistols placed between them, preventing any impropriety. Eventually, Moll entices him under the covers with the warning, 'Mind the pistols!'

In London, Mr Bland finds lodgings for Moll with Mrs Riordan. Moll tells him that he has 'tried the goods' and she now wants him to make her an offer for them, but Mr Bland has to admit that he is already married. Taking Moll to a tavern, he shows her his wife messing around with rough men.

But he eventually divorces her, weds Moll and they live happily for three years and have two children. Tragically, this period of stability in Moll's life ends when Mr Bland has a heart attack on hearing the news that he is bankrupt.

'He is very much a free-market warrior,' says James Fleet, who plays the dependable but slightly dull banker, 'a person who believes in the Conservative values of free enterprise and free markets. Bland is quite lascivious but, I think, very shy and awkward. He is a bit of a rumpy-pumpy man but needs the green light – and when he gets it, goes for it.'

James sees costumes and wigs as part and parcel of the actor's make-up, having performed in more than a dozen Royal Shakespeare Company productions, including the roles of Flute in *A Midsummer Night's Dream*, Peregrine in *Volpone* and Hortensio in *The Taming of the Shrew*, and worked with directors such as Trevor Nunn and Jonathan Miller.

He also played John Dashwood in Emma Thompson's screen adaptation of *Sense and Sensibility*. 'So putting all that clobber on in the morning for *Moll Flanders* was quite familiar,' he says. 'You sit and have your hair done for half an hour every morning and realise it's like being a woman – they go through this all the time.'

In the hit British film *Four Weddings and a Funeral*, James acted Tom, the seventh-richest man in England, and he has been a regular as Hugo in Dawn French's television sitcom *The Vicar of Dibley*. Both were written by

Richard Curtis. 'Richard has a fantastic ability to write stupid characters,' says James, 'and Hugo is the most stupid man in all of Dibley. Tom in *Four Weddings and a Funeral* was also stupid, but clever and kind, too.'

Lucy Diver
Nicola Walker

MOLL'S PARTNER-IN-CRIME Lucy Diver, 'the sharpest dip in England', is adapter Andrew Davies's composite of all those with whom Daniel Defoe's heroine worked in the original book. Moll first sees Lucy dressed up as a boy, running through the streets and throwing a bundle over a wall as people give chase, shouting, 'Stop, thief!' When the crowd has disappeared and the noise dies down, Moll picks up the bundle and adds the contents to her own proceeds of crime.

It is a surprise to Moll when she later finds Lucy sitting at the table in her own landlady's sitting room. The two hit it off immediately and team up, starting by stealing a jewelled watch from a pregnant woman at a concert hall recital. Lucy, who hates men, finds the companionship she is looking for with Moll, but Moll is devastated when her friend is caught red-handed in a market square stealing another jewelled watch and is sentenced to be hanged.

On the scaffold, Lucy makes a speech pointing out that she 'never hurt so much as a fly – what's a few watches and a few gold chains?' and exhorting her friends to 'tell everyone that Lucy Diver left this life with her head held high'.

Actress Nicola Walker, who plays Lucy, was adamant that she would do the hanging stunt herself. 'I think it's really noticeable in film and television scenes where they cut to a long-shot of an athletic-looking stuntwoman,' she says. 'The feeling of being suspended was the best thing.'

The stunt was co-ordinated by Nick Powell, a former actor who worked on the Mel Gibson film *Braveheart*, as well as *Robin Hood – Prince of Thieves* and *Batman*. The 'hangman's rope' was one piece of rope and a separate noose, with wires attached to a harness under Nicola's costume. 'The harness hurts under the crotch,' says Nicola, 'but it's no worse than being in a corset.' A stunt double was on hand to stand in if Nicola decided against doing the stunt herself, but was not needed.

Nicola had appeared in only a handful of television programmes before *Moll Flanders*, including episodes of *Faith* and *Milner*, as well as playing a sausage-seller and a boy in *Aristophanes*, for Channel Four. 'I play boys a lot,' she says. Nicola had the role of Claudia in *Four Weddings and a Funeral*, and, on stage, acted in three Royal Court Theatre productions and was directed by actor Martin Clunes in *Party Tricks* at Nottingham Playhouse.

Sir Richard Gregory
Ronald Fraser

ANDREW DAVIES created the role of drunken judge Sir Richard Gregory to give Moll the reprieve that saves her from the gallows and allows her to be transported to Virginia instead.

Moll meets Sir Richard in a tavern after watching the hanging of her friend Lucy Diver. He is the worse for drink but proposes a 'ride around the park in a coach' with Moll, and after having sex in the carriage, he falls asleep, allowing her to steal his gold watch, snuff box and other valuables. While Moll later waits to go to the gallows, Jemmy seeks Sir Richard to blackmail him into giving her a pardon, on pain of his wife being told what happened.

Since training at RADA in the early fifties, Ronald Fraser, who plays Sir Richard, has enjoyed a long career in theatre, film and television, and is often seen as the master of pomposity. His character roles on TV have included appearances in *Pennies from Heaven*, *Brideshead Revisited* and *Fortunes of War*, and he even starred in two sitcoms, playing Basil 'Badger' Allenby-Johnson, a rubber-planter returning from Malaya to find a very different England from the one he had left, in writer Roy Clarke's *The Misfit*, and the manic Inspector Spooner in the first series of Ray Galton and Johnny Speight's *Spooner's Patch*. More recently, the actor's upper-crust roles have included Judge MacVitie in an episode of *Class Act*, starring Joanna Lumley, and Sir Gregory Parsloe in P. G. Wodehouse's *Heavy Weather*.

In almost fifty films, Ronald has acted alongside such greats as Robert Mitchum, Deborah Kerr, Norman Wisdom, Laurence Harvey, David Niven, Harry Andrews, Richard Todd, Maurice Chevalier, Tony Hancock, Richard Burton, Elizabeth Taylor, James Stewart, Peter Finch and Ralph Richardson. In *Scandal*, Ronald played Justice Marshall, who tried Stephen Ward for living off the immoral earnings of prostitution in the Profumo affair of the sixties.

CHAPTER FOUR

DESIGN AND LOCATIONS

THE TASK OF FINDING suitable locations and creating the sets for *Moll Flanders* fell to production designer Stephen Fineren, who has worked on period dramas for Granada Television since the seventies. Series such as Catherine Cookson's *The Mallens, Cribb*, featuring Alan Dobie as the Victorian detective, and the acclaimed *Sherlock Holmes* stories, starring the late Jeremy Brett as Sir Arthur Conan Doyle's Victorian sleuth, all formed part of Stephen's broad experience in period dramas.

'Everything we had been doing for the previous twenty years had been eighteenth- or nineteenth-century and I was getting really bored with it,' recalls Stephen. 'Some time ago, I did a Restoration comedy, *The Double-Dealer*, written by William Congreve. It was a National Theatre production made by Granada at its Manchester studios and was directed by Peter Wood, who had directed the London stage play. Before Moll, that was my only excursion into the seventeenth century.'

The 1996 feature film *Moll Flanders* fixed the story firmly in the eighteenth century, but Stephen set to work on his research and was clear that the original was set a hundred years earlier. 'I read the Penguin Classics version of the book and tried to get as much information as I could from it,' he says. 'The most interesting part was the Notes section at the back. It gave a lot of detail about what Defoe was writing about in parts of the town and the historical significance of things that were happening.

'It's slightly unclear when the story was set – different people have different ideas. I started at the last page and worked backwards. Moll signed off her story in 1683, at the age of almost seventy. I then arrived at a date of about 1614 to start the story. I thought the story itself ended round about 1660. However, this was further complicated by the fact that the director intended to age Moll only into her mid-thirties.

'*Moll Flanders* was, I thought, a great opportunity to go back to Tudor times in terms of buildings and artefacts, and I wanted to weave in different historical and social details with the design. So I looked at the

Production designer Stephen Fineren, checking his sketches for the gallows set at the ruined castle, Rivington, was presented with the challenge of finding authentic seventeenth-century locations.

period from Henry VIII to Cromwell and Charles II. My visual cut-off point was the general introduction of the sash window – the Georgian style was something I didn't want to feature in any building or set, which is incredibly difficult when so much filming has to take place on location.

'If you look at obvious locations such as Stamford, where they filmed *Pride and Prejudice*, you are faced with lots of Georgian, Victorian and modern windows wherever you look. There weren't enough locations in terms of interrelated streets and houses to work for Episode 4, when Moll goes into houses, streets, back alleys, shops and pubs on a series of thieving missions. We couldn't satisfy those requirements in any way without building a complex set.'

A major event of British history marked a great change in the look of London shortly after the date at which Stephen envisaged the end of Granada's retelling of Moll's story. In 1666, the Great Fire destroyed more than 13,000 buildings, providing the architect Sir Christopher Wren with a remarkable opportunity to rebuild the city – but also giving any twentieth-century television production team a nightmare in recreating the old streets.

'Roy Jackson was used as location manager to look at various parts of the country that I thought might have possible exteriors and interiors,' says Stephen. 'Then a friend of mine in London said, "Sandwich, in Kent, is the ideal place." I didn't have time to go there, so he agreed to take photographs of the town and, after doing so, apologised, saying, "It's hopeless – it's full of Georgian windows!" We looked at Lavenham, Colchester, Ludlow and Lacock but, in the end, I realised that the only way we were going to get what we needed was to build a studio set and that was going to be expensive and beyond the existing budget.'

A certain amount of the filming of *Moll Flanders* had to take place in the Manchester region, within reach of Granada Television's studios, to prevent production costs from soaring. A former sports hall called Spectrum Arena, near Warrington, was used for all non-location filming. As well as the London streets complex, sets were built for shops, Newgate Prison, all the carriage interiors, the bedroom and living-room interiors and the ship's cabin, built on a rocker to give the motion needed.

Moll Flanders was an important production for Stephen. 'Every programme you do is a major production – it's the most important thing in your life at that point in time,' he says. 'But this one seemed to be the biggest, most important, most challenging drama that I have ever worked on.

'I approached it as if it were a mega-production. I was so ambitious about what I wanted to do, where I wanted to go for locations and what I would like to build. I wanted to get the very best locations, but it became more and more apparent that there were financial restrictions and we were restricted as to the number of days we were allowed to film away from the North West.

'My first question when starting work on a production is, "How much money have I got in the budget?" I'm asked to consider whether the design budget is achievable, do a complete breakdown of all the locations and put my knowledge to bear, saying I don't think we will find that, we will have to build that, we will have to decorate that house and so on.

'My initial, ambitious budget figure came to £1.2 million for sets, props, carriages, animals and special effects, and I was told that only £400,000 was allocated. When David Lascelles came on board as producer, I told him it was impossible to make it for this figure. Then we had bizarre conversations about it all being shot in close-up because that was all the budget could afford. I submitted a new budget based upon reduced ambitions and the realisation that more and more sets would have to be made on locations rather than as sets in the studio. That reduced my budget but increased the production costs.

'But we had to build a big street set and that was the clincher. I sketched out a plan of streets and alleyways, then produced three typical sketch elevations of buildings and had the whole scheme costed on a foot run basis. I could expect to get a 35ft two- to three-storey elevation for between £18,000 and £20,000, including scaffolding.

'I thought I needed £300,000 for that scheme alone. It was a design that filled the studio and went beyond the sports arena, out into the car park, so you got the impression of an extended street and a forced perspective.

'I was told this was far too expensive, so I cut the street back to about £250,000. That brought the whole of my costings down to £850,000. Eventually, we cut the street back to £200,000 by chopping out one side of it, and £100,000 was cut back from the other part of the budget, leaving me with a total final budget of just over £700,000, which eventually came down to £690,000. Also, the Granada Studios Tour agreed to buy the street set for £45,000 to put on display later. The Granada Group has got extremely good value for money.'

THE LOCATIONS

Smithills Hall, near Bolton

THE COURTROOM scene at the beginning of the first episode, where Moll's mother is sentenced to transportation and the baby is passed from hand to hand before going to live with gypsies, was filmed at Smithills Hall, near Bolton. The authentically restored fourteenth-century Great Hall fitted in perfectly with Stephen Fineren's ideas. 'I set the scene in an old medieval hall with crook beams,' he says. 'It has a very black-and-white, stark feel to it.'

Two interior scenes of the Golden Cock inn, where Moll first has a secret assignation with Rowland and later celebrates her wedding to his brother, were intended to be filmed at Smithills Hall. In the event, with just one day booked there, time ran out and they were shot with scenes inside another of Moll's bedrooms as part of the London streets composite set at Spectrum Arena, near Warrington.

The 'black-and-white, stark feel' of Smithills Hall provided the setting for a courtroom scene.

Church Street, in the Wiltshire village of Lacock, was converted into a seventeenth-century market town for the Colchester street scenes.

Church Street, Lacock

MOST OF THE SCENES in Episode 1 are set in the streets of Colchester, Essex, where eight-year-old Moll is taken in by Mr Richardson, the Mayor, and his family. Stephen took tiny Church Street, in the Wiltshire village of Lacock, and converted it into a market town of about 1630.

Because the real-life street is owned by the National Trust, all residents had to agree to Granada filming there and were paid a sum of money for enduring the inconvenience and disruption. They had become used to this when the BBC was filming Andrew Davies's adaptation of *Pride and Prejudice* there.

'I saw most of the buildings as being half-timbered, half-stone, with bits of brick here and there,' says Stephen. 'You could get a lot of that in Lacock, but we had to change all the doors and some of the windows, and paint the windows and both sides of the street. The biggest and most expensive transformation was the compacted stone-and-earth road surface.

'We set up a confectioner's and blacksmith's, and lots of commercial signs. Then we filled it with animals and carts and market stalls. The impression we wanted to give was a bustling market town. Among the animals were eight long-horn cattle – the original intention was to have more, but their sharp horns meant it could have been highly dangerous if they had stampeded down the narrow street.'

Packwood House, Warwickshire

FINDING AN AUTHENTIC exterior for the town house where Mayor Richardson would have lived in Colchester presented Stephen with a particular challenge. 'The problem with Defoe,' he says, 'is that he was setting the story in the seventeenth century but with the eighteenth century in mind, which was when he wrote it, so the house in the story was not a Tudor one. It was almost impossible to find a town house in a Tudor style that was situated in a town street – most were either country houses or modern commercial premises.'

Eventually, Stephen settled on Packwood House, a National Trust property between Warwick and Solihull. 'Initially, we went there to look at the garden because we had to find a location for Vauxhall Gardens for the walk Moll was to take with Dawkins,' he says. 'We used the gardens and came to the conclusion that the house itself looked interesting as a possible solution to the Richardsons' town house if we restricted the shooting to the frontage.'

Exteriors of the Richardson family's house were filmed at Packwood House, in Warwickshire.

The Granada Television team unload props and furniture at Castle Lodge, Ludlow.

Castle Lodge, Ludlow

INTERIORS FOR THE Richardson family's house were shot at Castle Lodge, Ludlow. 'I did recces throughout Shropshire, looking especially at Ludlow and Ledbury to see a couple of seventeenth-century houses I had researched that might be of use,' says Stephen. 'To be honest, I had ruled Ludlow out because I'd been there before and it was far too commercial. I looked at Church Street, in Ledbury, a gem of a place, like The Shambles, in York, but without shops. However, it was just a series of houses, pubs and a few tiny shops and it didn't really solve any of the story-telling problems, so we reluctantly decided not to shoot there.

'With an hour to spare, I decided to go to Ludlow to look at the castle there, to give us an exterior of Tyburn for the gallows scenes. Next to Ludlow Castle, which we didn't use in the end, was a house called Castle Lodge. A sign there said, "Historic House of Interest. £1." I walked through the door and it was fantastic – a whole series of empty rooms of fifteenth- or sixteenth-century origin. The structure was fifteenth-century, the panelling sixteenth-century.

'It was set on three floors and there were big stone fireplaces, oak panelling and rooms connected to each other with some arches, which was especially good for a sense of depth. The staircase was 4ft wide, twisting round, with poky passageways and interesting landings and ceilings. The top of the house was where the servants would have lived. It wasn't a classic historic house, just what I thought an established town house should be in the first half of the seventeenth century.

'Of course, there were many problems to be solved. Radiators had to be removed, pipework covered and grained into the panelling, electric lights and switches either covered or removed, carpets taken up and the staircase stained to look like dark oak. We then filled the house with furniture, tapestries, matting and drapes and, of course, many candles.'

Tatton Park, Cheshire

A FTER DISCOVERING Castle Lodge, Stephen travelled to Stokesay Castle, near Ludlow, which is owned by English Heritage. He hoped to turn the hall into the parish court and a solar room above it into a coaching inn bedroom. He also found the perfect spot there for Jemmy's prison cell.

'English Heritage said, "Fine, but no fires and no candles," and on this occasion we thought we could live with that,' recalls Stephen. 'Then, the week before we were due to start filming, someone from English Heritage who hadn't been consulted returned to his office and said "No filming," and those scenes were due to be done during that first week of the shooting schedule. I had already propped all the furniture and dressings, and built all the window shutters.'

This setback meant that the schedule had to be changed and new locations found. Stephen found a tythe barn in Little Moreton Hall, near Congleton, complete with cattle. Unfortunately, the farmer died two weeks before Granada was due to start filming and his wife did not want it to go ahead.

The medieval tythe barn at Tatton Park was used for filming the parish court.

'We were running out of medieval tythe barns,' says Stephen. 'The only other one I knew was the one at Tatton Hall – which, strangely enough, was given to Tatton Park by the person I bought my house off! So that's where we filmed the parish court.'

Astley Hall, Chorley

Two bedroom scenes were filmed at Astley Hall – one with Moll and Dawkins after the draper's party, the other Mr Bland's death-bed scene.

STEPHEN WAS STILL left with new locations to find after his run of bad luck. He already knew of Astley Hall, at Astley Park, near Chorley, in Lancashire, and realised that it was one of the few places in the area that would provide enough sets for a full day's filming.

It became the town house of Mr Bland, Moll's fifth husband. One bedroom was used for his death scene, while another was used for the bedroom scene that Moll shares with Dawkins, her second husband, after the party he gives in his draper's shop.

This house presented the usual problems of wall-painting, stair carpets, staining, panelling, electric light fittings and radiators – all the negative things that have to be removed or hidden before the place can be brought alive with furnishings.

The George Inn, Norton St Philip

A SETTING FOR THE Mint, the debtors' retreat where Moll seeks accommodation after Dawkins leaves for France with the bailiffs on his doorstep, was found at The George Inn, in Norton St Philip, Somerset. 'The interior location in the roof space was good to start with,' says Stephen, 'and all I needed to do was to partition it off with broken-down wattle-and-daub panels, and dress three different bedrooms as really shabby, run-down apartments. We used the exterior and internal yard as the Lancashire coaching inn seen before Moll goes to the fictional High Peaks Hall.'

Cornwall

THE NAUTICAL PARTS of *Moll Flanders* were filmed in Cornwall. These included quayside scenes set in Chatham and Milford Haven, as well as those when Moll arrives in the harbour at Virginia with her third husband, sea captain Lemuel, and later leaves without him.

'I did a recce of the River Fal,' recalls Stephen. 'I was taken to various landing stages down the river, looking for locations. We came across a pub-restaurant, which local sources thought was the best possibility for me, but the river had too many moored, redundant ships and the *King Harry* ferry would probably have appeared in the middle of the shot. I chatted to the owner of the restaurant and he suggested a spot down the coast called Turnaware Point, where there is an old American D-Day landing stage.

'There was no access there except by foot. I had to walk about half a mile to it and it turned out to be perfect – not a ship in sight. There was just an eighteenth-century stately home on top of a hill that we could avoid. The landing stage was completely overrun with branches, bracken, gorse and grass. We had to have the consent of the National Trust and its approval to knock down a stone wall that blocked the access down to the landing stage.

'Local contractors built an 80ft-long by 10ft-wide jetty out into the River Fal. All the quayside buildings had been scaffolded. We spent two days erecting the scenery and building a slave hut. At the same time, the prop crew were dressing the usual cotton bales, crates, animal pens, barrels and furniture along the jetty and quayside. I had twelve tobacco barrels made by a Liverpool barrel maker because I couldn't find any of the right size and detail to hire.'

Turnaware Point, on the River Fal, was an authentic spot for filming Moll and Lemuel's arrival in Virginia, where the happy couple are met by his mother, Mrs Golightly (Diana Rigg).

For the scenes intended to represent Chatham, from where Lemuel's ship sets sail for America, Charlestown Harbour, near St Austell, proved a good location. Two boats were used for the filming there. The *Santa Maria*, which had previously appeared in director Ridley Scott's feature film *1492: Conquest of Paradise*, telling the story of Christopher Columbus's epic voyage across the Atlantic to America, was hired by Granada from a company called Square Sail. The boat was originally built in 1929 as a Danish Evangelical Mission schooner, and in 1976, refitted as a brigantine and called *The Phoenix*, won the American Bicentennial Tall Ships Race in its class. Square Sail, which is dedicated to the preservation of historical ships, bought the boat in 1988 and completely refitted it.

The *Santa Maria* was repanelled and repainted to become Lemuel's transportation ship, which was filmed at both Turnaware Point and Charlestown Harbour, where the *Earl of Pembroke* was also hired from Square Sail to place in the background so that its rigging and masts could be seen. Although the hull shape was more eighteenth-century than the *Santa Maria*, it was useful filmed head-on to create a busy quayside feel.

Lincolnshire

THE FLATLANDS OF Lincolnshire became an obvious location for the Virginia scenes. 'We knew we had to go to Lincolnshire,' says Stephen, 'because it has wide-open fields and is so different from anywhere else.

'My research and information from the Lucas Film Library in America and research done by Sue Swingler, a freelance, at the American Institute here was that the early English settlers in America took craftsmen builders over with them and built a style of architecture that was known to them. At the time of our story, that was late-Elizabethan. Most of the furnishings were taken over from England historically, but we tried to give more of a New World feel to the interiors. I wanted to make the sets feel much more modern and clean than anything in England.'

The Red Hall, at Bourne, believed to have been built as early as 1595 and now owned by a charitable trust, was used for interior and exterior filming of Plantation House, where Moll lives with Lemuel and his mother.

'When I went to look at the Red Hall,' recalls Stephen, 'it was surrounded by modern houses – all you could do outside was to shoot

LEFT: The Red Hall, at Bourne, was used for filming interior and exterior scenes of Plantation House, in Virginia.

BELOW: Scenes of the Virginia tobacco plantations were filmed on land around Grimsthorpe Castle, near Bourne.

The redundant church of St George's, Goltho, is the setting for the Virginia church scenes.

straight on – but inside it was pretty good. There was a panelled room that was painted grey-blue, which I thought was perfect for a totally different "modern" look, and we painted the whole of the Jacobean staircase in grey and cream. The long gallery at the top of the house was a beautiful space, which we dressed as an extended drawing room-cum-playroom-cum-music room, and kept it all cool, with simple oak furniture and cream muslin drapes.'

For the tobacco plantations themselves, Granada filmed on land around Grimsthorpe Castle, near Bourne, which had previously been used for television productions of *Middlemarch* and *The Buccaneers*. 'In some paintings of the period,' says Stephen, 'I saw guard huts in the middle of the plantations. Because of problems with the Indians, they had shacks and shelters built on stilts above the crops, so I built four of those. It was a detail not seen in the English landscape.'

The Virginia church scenes were shot at St George's, in Goltho, a remote, redundant brick-built church, matching Stephen's seemingly impossible specifications. The church is located in one of Lincolnshire's lost villages, along the main Lincoln-Wragby road, a site that was excavated in the seventies. The building is the only remains of an ancient village whose centre was deserted in the middle of the fourteenth century, although the nave and chancel are believed to have been added in the sixteenth and seventeenth centuries.

The interior of St George's Church was painted a pale blue that matched perfectly the colours of Plantation House, a panelled wall was added between the congregation and the altar, and some extra pews were built. The familiar image of clapboard churches and houses with colon-naded frontages and pedimented doorways was a later development in American buildings.

Little Moreton Hall, Congleton

Three different tavern scenes were filmed at Little Moreton Hall, a moated manor house near Congleton, in Cheshire, noted for its timber-framed architecture, dating back to the fifteenth century and now owned by the National Trust: the stairs, bedroom and dining room at Westchester Inn, where Moll and Jemmy stay on their honeymoon; the 'pistols bedroom' where Mr Bland sits on guard with his guns while Moll goes to bed; and the staircase and bed-chamber of the coaching inn at Ware, where Jemmy arrives while Moll is honeymooning there with Bland. The courtyard was used for the shots of Moll and Bland arriving at the inn.

'The timber there was old and mellow but not too ancient – it had the right feel for a coaching inn,' says Stephen. 'It seemed an ideal location because we could put our own furnishings into the various rooms. All the prop and scenery lorries arrived in convoy at the appointed time, but this was a house that was open to the public until 5p.m. As soon as the last member of the public left, we were allowed to drive up and off-load the props and work through two nights before filming.

'I had to paint all the rooms and hang tapestries with wires and wedges and sky hooks. The curator, Stephen Adams, was an absolute delight to work with. Once we had established what the National Trust wanted, the co-operation we got locally was superb. The wall-painting was done to give a much more broken, shabby feel to the rooms. After filming, all these rooms had to be repainted in the standard National Trust cream.'

Little Moreton Hall was also the setting for the scenes of Dawkins's party in his draper's shop. Stephen re-dressed the tavern in the Great Hall, built a series of tall draper's frames with rotating bolts of silk on them and placed a big cutting table down the middle of the room.

The timber-framed architecture of Little Moreton Hall provided the right feel for a coaching inn.

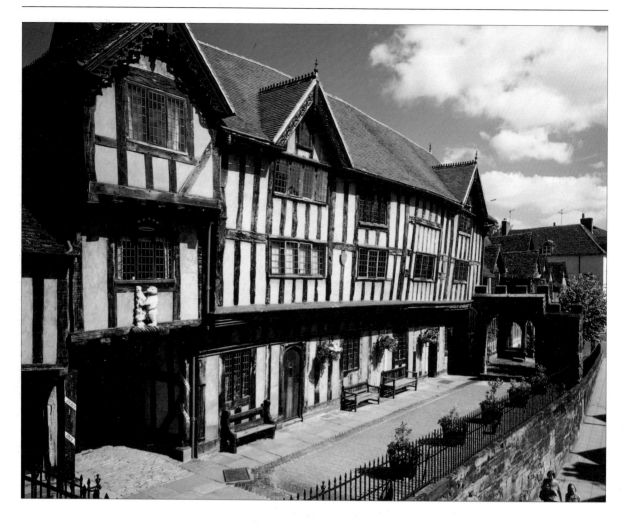

Lord Leycester Hospital, Warwick

The half-timbered Lord Leycester Hospital, in Warwick, was used for exterior shots of Westchester Inn.

THE EXTERIOR OF Westchester Inn was filmed at the Lord Leycester Hospital, in Warwick High Street, which dates back to the fourteenth century and was bought by the Earl of Leycester – an influential figure at the court of Elizabeth I – in 1571 as a home for old and disabled soldiers and their wives. It is now a self-supporting charity, getting most of its income from visitors.

'To me,' says Stephen, 'this is one of the most interesting half-timbered buildings in England. The colouring and texture of the plaster and oak beams is absolutely beautiful and perfect for yet another coaching inn. Other than laying another soil-and-sand surface over the road and courtyard and the panelling-over of some ancient crests, the building itself was virtually unaltered, once we had removed the light fittings, double glazing and window dressings!'

Haddon Hall, Bakewell

GETTING TO USE Haddon Hall, near Bakewell, in Derbyshire, fulfilled an ambition for Stephen. 'It's in my repertoire of locations I always wanted to use but had never been able to,' he says. 'It's a two-hour journey from Granada and overnight stays are expensive, so we had to pick the best, most important locations very carefully.'

It provided enough interiors and exteriors for five days' filming. The Great Hall was used for the ballroom scene in which Moll is introduced to Jemmy, and a drawing-room sequence where a Catholic priest chats to Moll before taking her confession was partially filmed here and the confession itself filmed against a perspex and polystyrene window in the studio.

In the story, the confession is followed by Moll's marriage to Jemmy. The intention was to film the wedding ceremony at Astbury Church, near Congleton, but this was rapidly rethought after Stephen checked this for historical authenticity.

'Until Ron Pritchard, the production buyer, asked questions of the Catholic Church about the sort of dressings they had at the time for wedding services,' he says, 'none of us had considered that there were no official Catholic weddings because they were illegal under the Church of

Haddon Hall, in Derbyshire, provided enough interiors and exteriors for five days' filming.

England! Any weddings would be in the Church of England or undercover by a friendly Catholic priest.

'We had set up an interior at Astbury Church for the grand wedding when the penny dropped. I suggested having the wedding in a barn, which is what we eventually did, but not at Haddon Hall because this would have exceeded our overnight locations' budget. We found a barn at Hoghton Tower, in Lancashire, which solved this problem.

'Because there were no churches, there were no confessionals either, so we had to invent how to do that scene as well. There was a lovely bay window at the end of the drawing room at Haddon Hall. I thought it would be a good place for the priest to hear Moll's confession. I used an embroidery frame with stretched muslin on, which would act as a fine screen between the priest and Moll. Unfortunately, we couldn't shoot the scene at Haddon Hall because we ran out of time. All we did was the wide shot of her going into the window and the rest we re-created in the studio.'

A room upstairs from the drawing room at Haddon Hall was used for the scene where Moll meets a group of sea captains, including her husband-to-be, Lemuel. This was set in the Maritime Club at Chatham, to which Moll travels after her

OPPOSITE: The Great Hall at Haddon Hall was used for filming the colourful country ball at which Moll meets Jemmy.

ABOVE: An open-air theatre scene
and the courtroom where Moll and
Lucy Diver are sentenced to death
were both filmed at Hoghton Tower.

second husband, Dawkins, flees the country. 'In the original story,' says Stephen, 'it was set in a drawing room, but we decided to make it into a maritime club because it would be more interesting visually. I filled it with globes, charts, models of galleons and paintings of warships, and made it the nautical equivalent of a gentlemen's club.'

Haddon Hall's kitchens were transformed into a city-centre tavern where Moll meets the drunken judge, Sir Richard Gregory, whose indiscretion with her eventually leads to her escaping the gallows. The tavern is also where Mr Bland's first wife is seen cavorting with other men.

'We set both scenes in the same tavern and said it was probably the most popular tavern in the town,' says Stephen. 'One of the things that I tried to do was to give some colour definition to various locations. If I had kept to the tired colour of washed-out ochre, it would soon have got repetitive. A lot of these locations look very similar and there was the risk of making everything look exactly the same.

'So I decided to go for much stronger colours than we would normally go for on the assumption that most of the rooms are full of smoke, which tends to desaturate the colours anyway. I put quite a strong bottle green in the tavern, based upon a Dutch painting I found of a tavern dated 1650.'

Hoghton Tower, near Blackburn

THE COURTYARD AT Hoghton Tower, near Blackburn, in Lancashire, was used for an open-air theatre scene because Stephen could not find or afford to build a Restoration theatre. The barn became the setting for Moll and Jemmy's wedding ceremony, the Catholic wedding that has to be held in secret. The barn was filled with hay, and candlesticks were added to give the atmosphere of a rural wedding.

'The barn interior seemed to me perfect for a private but atmospheric occasion,' says Stephen. 'It reminded me of Le Corbusier's chapel

at Ronchamp, with its small, square windows cut into the walls so that sunlight shines across in beams of bright light.'

A third set provided by Hoghton Tower was the courtroom where both Moll and her friend Lucy Diver are sentenced to be hanged in different parts of the story. 'I built that as a set within the banqueting hall,' says Stephen. 'My research showed that they made courts in halls, with a travelling dock, a travelling judge's bench and lots of seating for the jurors and the barristers. The well was filled with clerks' benches and hangers-on. In the seventeenth century, a court case was a huge social event.'

Stephen re-dressed the courtroom to double as a concert hall for a recital at which Moll and Lucy knock over a pregnant woman and steal her jewelled watch. He filled the set with benches, pews, flowers and candles. 'We wanted to shoot this in Oxford with two other street scenes,' he says, 'but the travelling and the cost of hiring the halls and churches and chapels was too expensive.'

A scene where Moll's second husband, Dawkins, takes her to an open-air theatre at night was also filmed at Hoghton Tower. The set, which Stephen based on an illustration of an Italian travelling theatre, had to be rebuilt later at the back of Spectrum Arena to complete filming of the scene.

A barn at Hoghton Tower, with shafts of light shining through the small, square windows, was a perfect setting for Moll and Jemmy's wedding.

Roddlesworth Reservoir, near Bolton

THE SCENE FOR Jemmy's 'stand and deliver' scene, where he holds up a stagecoach that has his wife Moll inside – to the surprise of both of them – was filmed at Roddlesworth Reservoir, in the Lancashire countryside between Bolton and Blackburn. This was a location that Mick Graham, one of the location managers on the production, was given the task of finding after he returned from scouting the Virginian landscapes in Lincolnshire.

Rivington Castle, near Bolton

The ruined castle at Rivington provided the perfect set for both Lucy Diver and Moll's hanging scenes.

TYBURN, the historic execution site near Marble Arch, in London, but in the rough, scrubby countryside during the seventeenth century, was the setting for two parts of the story – the hanging of Lucy Diver, for petty theft, and Moll's own gallows scene.

'I had seen an illustration by Hogarth depicting Tyburn, which was one of only two illustrations we could find,' says Stephen. 'The building next to it wasn't a castle – it was a ruined house. I think Hogarth used it and romanticised it to make an interesting profile. I was happy to go along with that.'

After many problems in coming up with a suitable location, it was decided less than a week before the day's shoot to use the ruined castle on the shores of Lower Rivington Reservoir, near Bolton. It is, in fact, a replica of Liverpool Castle, which was demolished in 1725. The copy was built almost two centuries later by the late Lord Leverhulme, who wanted to show what the original looked like after the spoils of the Civil War.

Spectrum Arena, near Warrington

THE COMPOSITE London streets set, with its interior shops and apartments, and that for Newgate Prison were built at Spectrum Arena, a former sports hall at Birchwood, near Warrington. They cost almost one-third of the entire production design budget, although Stephen's ambitions had already been scaled down to meet the budget. One side of a street was not built and extra money was gained by securing agreement from Granada Studios Tours to buy the set for £45,000 after the production to include alongside its other attractions at the television studios in Manchester.

'The problem of construction was enormous,' says Stephen. 'All three contractors that we used each had to build one or more areas of the set. No single contractor could have built even half of it in the time given. They just managed to build it in the four weeks allocated, but everything was rushed and compromised.

'Tim Farmer, my second art director, was given the task of developing and drawing all the exteriors from original sketches, photographs and prints by myself and Alan Price. He supervised the building and installation of the set with construction manager Brian Eatough and production buyer David Round.

'After filming finished in Cornwall, I came back to look at the sets and my first art director, Alan Price, supervised the Lincolnshire part of the shoot. When I arrived, I found that the wood-graining wasn't up to the usual standard and some of the painting of the oak half-timbered buildings was rushed and poorly executed. Two of the contractors' painters were called back to finish off the job to our satisfaction.'

All the leaded windows were intended to have a very fine coating of French enamel in shades of amber, green and blue, all mottled and giving a slightly distorted look. But Stephen found that some of the most

important windows were looking
milky and he was unable to see in
or out. He had the windows
stripped down with cellulose
thinner, and much purer French
enamel coating was applied with
sponges to create that early
coloured glass look that is so different from nineteenth- and twentieth-century glass.

'I'm happy with the final
result,' says Stephen, 'but it took
some effort to finish it off and
co-ordinate. Each contractor
approached the making and painting of oak beams in different
ways, but this generates buildings
that are dissimilar and, in some
instances, unreal. In the final
analysis, I believe the most suc-
cessful technique is to use an adze
[a cutting tool with an arched
blade set at right angles to the
handle] on rough, unplaned timber boards, torch them with a
flame-thrower and wash over with
ochre paint and finish off with a
series of walnut and black colour
washes.'

The graveyard where Moll
takes a little girl and steals her
necklace was created as part of
the overall streets' set. It sloped up
to a church, going up above the
blacksmith's yard and on to a bal-
cony 10ft beyond the studio wall,
which enabled Stephen to back-
light the windows of the church
and create a greater feeling of
depth.

The set for Newgate Prison

The walls and arches of the Newgate Prison set, for Moll and Jemmy's gaol scenes, were re-used in the London streets set.

was built on a large scaffolding rig 6ft in the air so that Moll's cell would look 6ft underground in a pit. The prison scenes were filmed first at Spectrum so that the walls and arches could then be dismantled and most of them used in the streets set, which was filmed four weeks later. This created a budget saving of up to £30,000.

Four shops that appear in the production were created out of two different sets. 'I designed the shelving for the pawnbroker's as units that would split and reassemble in a different form,' says Stephen. 'There was a sequence in the draper's shop that we filmed at Little Moreton Hall. I made tall racks with bolts of fine silk and designed them to be re-used in the mercer's shop on the streets set. The whole of the mercer's shop is full of scenery that has appeared in other scenes.'

PROPS

THOUSANDS OF PROPS were needed for the production's 275 scenes, from small items such as jewellery and clay pipes to horses and carriages. For the horses and carriages, Granada went to Stephen Dent, who runs his father's old firm outside London, which used to supply Pinewood and Shepperton Studios in the heyday of the British film industry.

'I knew he would have all the agricultural carts we needed,' says designer Stephen Fineren, 'but I had a feeling he wouldn't have any seventeenth-century carriages — and he didn't. We did some research on what the carriages would have looked like and found ourselves looking at illustrations just a quarter-of-an-inch high which were just a small part of landscape and townscape paintings.

'For the three important carriages that featured heavily, we knew we had to build the interiors with break-away panels, so we built them all in one: the London stagecoach; Mrs Seagrave's carriage that takes Moll to the dance and away on her wedding night to Jemmy; and a London

cab. Alan Price and Nick Wilkinson completed the designs and drawings of the three principal carriages. Each carriage was then repanelled
and painted in different colours. If it was an open carriage in one scene,
I made it a closed one in the next. If it was red, I made it green. Each
one went through at least three changes of identity until in the end I was
confused!

'Stephen Dent then rebuilt three carriages that he had already used
on medieval films. They were covered in sackcloth and rope, so he
stripped all that and repanelled them and applied brass studs, repainted
them and put leather pelmets around the roofs. In all, I had ten of
Stephen Dent's original carriages, which were used several times each,
and built three totally authentic seventeenth-century carriages that he
has since bought from us.'

Many animals were used in the production. For just one scene filmed
at Charlestown Harbour, doubling as Chatham, there were ten geese,
twenty-four chickens, six cattle, six sheep and one pig, and even they
were not enough!

Food provided another challenge for the production team.

The three principal carriages used in
Moll Flanders were designed by Alan
Price and Nick Wilkinson, and more
were created by repanelling and
repainting them.

Researching what families would eat in the seventeenth century, food stylist Debbie Brodie came up with the following supper menu for seven for the well-to-do Richardson household in the first episode:

1. Platter of oysters (to eat)
2. Rare chine of beef (dressing)
3. Spinach dressed with eggs (to eat)
4. Great dish of roasted fowl (to eat)
5. Pippin tart (dressing)
6. Hash of rabbits (dressing)
7. Fruit and cheese (to eat)

For another scene with twelve people, she gave them the following supper:

1. Baked stuffed salmon (dressing)
2. Quails (to eat)
3. Dish of artichokes (to eat)
4. Pears (to eat)
5. Salt fish pie with sweet spices (dressing)
6. Tart of damsons (dressing)
7. Peas in oil (to eat)
8. Mallard smothered (dressing)
9. Grand salad, decorated with branches of rosemary (to eat)

Throughout, Stephen Fineren tried to depict everything as authentically as possible. During a two-week holiday before Christmas 1995, he even spent most of his time researching the period and coming up with a document entitled *Period Notes 1550-1680* to distribute to his art directors and production buyers.

It included such gems as: 'Large beds were common – everybody slept in the same one . . . Bedchambers were used for entertaining . . . Tapestries were many in wealthy houses . . . One knife minimum per working-class family . . . Tobacco was sold in shops at over 30s. [£1.50] a pound (1603) – very expensive . . . Mirrors were not large until late seventeenth century . . . Every shop had its hanging sign on wrought-iron brackets.' Apparently, these signs were banned in the eighteenth century because too many were falling down on people in the streets, and the fascia sign then came into its own.

FURNITURE AND FABRICS

STEPHEN FINEREN and production buyer Ron Pritchard travelled to London hire companies to look for furniture and fabrics for *Moll Flanders* with a briefcase full of drawings and lists. Within five days, they had hired every available piece of furniture, fabric, painting and artefact suitable for the period – some of it reproduction – but had still only a quarter of what they needed. This meant reusing what they already had.

Furnishing one of the many bedroom sets was complicated by staircase access if they were on location. 'Four-poster beds don't dismantle very easily and, on many occasions, we used two

demountable beds that we manufactured ourselves,' says Stephen. 'Each bedroom would then require six bed drapes, a bed cover and up to six window drapes. To repeat this more than twenty times became a massive problem, solved to some extent by buying period fabrics from John Lewis, or directly from Warners and Mulberry, and having them made up.

'The most luxurious fabrics were the tapestries from Brussels, followed by the cheaper Tapisseries de Bergamo and the simple, decorative hanging that was painted on to linen or woollen cloth. I only ever used carpet as table coverings – they were normally Turkish, Anatolian-style rugs. The floors, if covered, would have been rush matting sewn together in strips to suit each room size. Other more feminine or sensual dressing tables were covered in embroidered or appliquéd cloths.

'Most of the windows and bed drapes were of damask. Some were of silk, but usually linen or wool. Bed linings and sun curtains were in taffeta, which is a plain silk weave. Although flock fabrics and wallpapers were available from the time of Charles II, I decided not to use wallpaper at all because this would have been a more eighteenth-century fashion accessory than a seventeenth-century reality.'

Hanging signs were common during the seventeenth century, and scenic artist Richard Brockless recreates one for *Moll Flanders*.

CHAPTER FIVE

COSTUMES, HAIR AND MAKE-UP

COSTUMES

IN A PERIOD DRAMA, costumes help to create the overall look. Costume dramas have also proved big money-spinners for British television companies, with sales worldwide of series and serials such as *The Six Wives of Henry VIII*, *Elizabeth R*, *The Onedin Line* and *The Duchess of Duke Street*. All of those were made in the seventies, but the eighties saw their demise after Granada Television's lavishly mounted serials *Brideshead Revisited* and *The Jewel in the Crown*, whose production values proved a high point in British television history.

In the nineties, the popularity of the BBC's *Middlemarch* and *Pride and Prejudice* signalled a return to costume drama, and Granada Television was determined that it would make *Moll Flanders* as good as anything the BBC could do, if not better.

The job of designing costumes for *Moll Flanders* went to Trisha Biggar, who had previously worked with director David Attwood on the film *Wild West* and the Screen Two television movie *Saigon Baby*, so she was already used to being presented with a challenge.

Trisha had just six weeks' preparation for *Moll Flanders* before filming started. She read the book and the scripts, talked to David Attwood about the characters and hired one researcher in London and another in America.

'As this is such an early period, there are only a few surviving pieces of seventeenth-century clothing,' says Trisha. 'All our ideas of what people wore then have to come from paintings, etchings, letters and diaries of the time. Using these sources, I researched colours of fabrics, textile design and embroidery. With paintings, I had to be aware that there was very little interest in portraying the social conditions of the lower classes and most painters earned their living from commissions from the Church or upper classes, who wanted family portraits often depicting their life in an idealised or allegorical way – sometimes for the most

Costume designer Trisha Biggar, who had just six weeks to prepare for *Moll Flanders*, was able to reflect the fact that the seventeenth century was a time of great change in men's and women's fashion.

The flamboyant Daniel Dawkins
(Christopher Fulford), Moll's second
husband, wore petticoat breeches in
the Restoration era.

simple reason that when fashion changed their pictures wouldn't look dated.

'Obviously, I had to use some licence. For example, our research at Greenwich Maritime Museum showed that the Navy hadn't issued uniforms at this time. It was in 1746 that naval officers decided they wanted to wear a uniform, as other nations had started to do so. Previously, naval captains could wear what they liked. There was no official uniform issued to ordinary seamen actually working the boats before the mid-nineteenth century, either. They had to buy what were known as slops, which were available on board, and the cost was deducted from the seamen's pay when the voyage was over.

'The seventeenth century was one of great change, for men and women. My costumes start from about 1650 and go to 1700. I tried to give each episode a different feel, a slightly different silhouette, because fashion was changing so much during that century. I was able to divide up the four episodes into four loose costume periods.

'Fashions evolved throughout the seventeenth century. For women during the first three-quarters of the century, a softer, more rounded silhouette developed. The very low oval necklines — showing a lot of cleavage — and heavily boned and stiffened bodices of the middle part of the century gradually gave way from about 1680 to the narrower silhouette and squarer necklines of the less constricting gowns that were known as mantuas.

'Pleating was used to mould the fabric to the body in the bodice, and then the fabric was allowed to fall in folds to form the skirt, which was open down the centre front and draped up over the hips or looped up to the centre back to allow the decorated petticoat to be seen. The mantua was worn over "stays", or corsets, which were decorated or covered by a separate embellished stomacher, which sometimes matched the petticoat.'

Changes to men's clothes throughout the century were more radical. 'They started the century in doublets and breeches,' says Trisha, 'and progressed through what were known as petticoat breeches – as worn by Moll's second husband, Dawkins – to, by about 1670, narrow and straight knee-length coats with waistcoats, which in the following decades gained volume in the skirt as fullness was added to the sides.

'By 1700, this extra fullness was beginning to be controlled by pleating at the side seams below the hip line. The fashion for leaving the skirt seams open continued for almost the next hundred years to accommodate the sword, with the hilt coming through the side vent and the point through the centre back vent. Pocket levels and sleeve and cuff lengths varied as the coat evolved.'

Trisha had a clear vision of how she wanted everything to look. 'By emphasising colour, fabric and change in fashion,' she says, 'I could reflect some of the changes in Moll's life. I gave the early part of the story, set in Colchester, a Puritan feel, using sombre colours and Puritan collars to suggest demureness. This was a time when personal extravagance was discouraged and modesty and constraint were advocated – at least on the surface.

'Moll then arrives in London at the beginning of the Restoration era to start life afresh, free from the constraints of a loveless marriage, during a period of colourful flamboyance and lavishness. For the American section, I used more earthy colours and lighter-weight fabrics to suggest heat, to contrast with England.'

Trisha had a budget of about £100,000 and used a total of 1,500 costumes for the production. Of these, 1,100 were for extras in crowd scenes and 400 were for the principal actors and actresses, of which a hundred were specially made, including almost forty alone for Moll. The renowned London company Angels & Bermans supplied or made most of the costumes and Trisha hired a few from other sources.

'Staying within the budget is always important,' she says, 'and often involves compromises by all departments. Having done a rough breakdown before detailed discussions with the producer and director, I then revised it after establishing with David Attwood how he planned to shoot various scenes. I worked out how many costumes would need to be doubled to cover stunt sequences or to signify a passage of time to the audience. For instance, when Moll is arrested and imprisoned in Newgate, we used four versions of the same outfit in various states of deterioration. From the scripts, I worked out how many principal actors would be cast and how many costumes each actor would need, and how much that would leave to spend on extras.

'When Alex Kingston was cast as Moll, I hadn't made any definite decisions about colours for her costumes before meeting her because an actress's own colouring, shape and opinion on how she sees the character is very important. When we met, I showed her various designs and fabric samples, and we discussed the script and what she would be doing in each outfit. For instance, if she had to undress in shot, how it could be done easily, or if she was to be walking in the countryside we would make a dress without a train.

'Obviously, some costumes can be used in more than one scene, but others such as wedding or ball dresses cannot, athough we decided as a deliberate thing to have Moll wear the same ball dress that she wears when she falls in love with Jemmy as she wears when Jemmy finally rescues her from the gallows and they set off for a new and happy life together.'

Trisha was also responsible for hats, gloves, jewellery and baldricks, in which swords are held. Hats were high in the Puritan period, lower in the Restoration era. Moll has fifteen hats throughout the four-hour production. Gloves were specially made for Moll, Jemmy, Sir Richard Gregory and various other actors. 'They were quite elaborate in that period,' says Trisha, 'high gauntlet gloves in soft leather with lots of decoration.'

For the American scenes, Moll does not wear a hat, but Lemuel's mother has a close-fitting white bonnet. 'We wanted to keep a look of freedom for Moll,' says Trisha. 'Life was good and she was enjoying it. When she comes back to England, Moll has a red velvet hat that matches her red dress. In Episode 4, she wears fontanges, which are tall, and complement the lower, narrower shape of the dresses.'

Polaroid photographs used in continuity during filming to ensure that costume details were correct.

1. Alex Kingston starts off as the eighteen-year-old Moll in a very simple black Puritan linen dress that mirrors the one worn by Young Moll at the age of seven, with similar shape and fabric.

As the story progresses and Moll becomes attracted to Rowland, the Puritan shape remains. There was always a lot of cleavage, but Puritan collars, particularly during the years of Oliver Cromwell, were used to cover up.

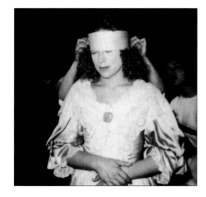

2. For Moll's first wedding, to Robin, she wears a dress with a bit more colour than she is previously seen in. It is still very simple, to retain the Puritan look, but gives her a youthful appearance. It is a peach satin dress with brocade underskirt and white flowery chemise.

3. The dress Moll wears when she sees Jemmy for the first time, on her arrival in London, is pink with a gold floral pattern that catches the light. This dress was originally made for the 1996 film *Restoration*.

4. The ivory silk dress for Moll's wedding to Dawkins, complete with embroidered bodice and front panels, silver thread embroidery, pearls and gold beads, is worn with a pale blue silk hooded cape.

'Moll thought at that point that she was marrying someone with money,' says Trisha. 'Her wedding dresses throughout the production change depending on how much money she thinks her husband has and how much he believes she has!'

5. Another dress from the film *Restoration* is used in the television production for the theatre scene with Dawkins. It is made of gold fabric with gold piping and large puff sleeves, and Moll wears it with matching underskirt.

6. When Moll rushes off to Chatham after Dawkins flees the bailiffs, she spends what money she has on clothes. After she meets sea captain Lemuel, he is soon undressing her aboard his ship. This posed particular problems for Trisha.

'We had to make the outfit so that it opens easily in front of the camera,' she says, 'and it had to look feasible. Most of the dresses of the period didn't open down the front, only down the back, so we made a pale blue silk-and-linen dress with blue bows all the way down the front that undo. We added a blue corset underneath that looks very pretty when the dress is undone.'

7. The American scenes presented Trisha with the challenge of providing Moll with a totally different look. 'I put her into much simpler, less decorated clothes,' she says, 'and used linens, cottons and corduroys, as well as keeping the colours more muted. Green was a very popular colour in America at the time. Everyone was wearing green stockings, according to written references we found. Also, I wanted to keep that section in softer colours and lighter-weight fabrics to give a feel of heat.'

8. Arriving back in England after leaving Lemuel, Moll looks a mess as a result of the storm on the boat journey home, so she goes into a shop and buys the dress that she wears on her subsequent stage coach journey, when she meets Jemmy. A stunt double was needed for this dress because Moll wears it later when out riding with Jemmy.

'It is in slightly stronger colours and more decorated, a dark red velvet dress with old gold braid and red ribbons, with an orange and gold underskirt – a seventeenth-century version of riding habit,' says Trisha. 'She is back in England and has spent what money she has to catch her husband. She sets off in this outfit with a dark red velvet hat to match.'

9. The lilac and silver dress with maroon bows and silver puff sleeves that Moll wears at the ball with Jemmy is the same one that she has on for her gallows scene. Costume designer Trisha Biggar dressed the rest of the people at the ball in slightly duller colours, apart from Mrs Seagrave, Jemmy's supposed sister but in reality his former lover, who wears a deep turquoise-blue colour.

'It was meant to be a small county ball with local gentry, not high fashion,' says Trisha. 'I kept everyone else low-key, in softer colours because I wanted Moll to make an entrance. She arrives in a dark burgundy cloak with gold yoke and fur trim.'

10. Moll marries Jemmy in a very heavily decorated dress of embroidered gold gauze with an embossed gold underskirt. The fabric for the underskirt came from India and Trisha spotted just a four-metre panel of it in a shop in Notting Hill, West London. 'Normally, you need ten metres,' explains Trisha, 'so we used cotton at the back, which was done during that period. Then, as now, exquisite fabric was very expensive. This was the most important wedding costume for me because Jemmy is important in her life and Moll spends a lot of time in it.'

11. For her wedding to Mr Bland, Moll wears a much plainer silk dress in pale green, with a cream and green patterned underskirt, simpler in terms of decoration but not shape.

12. Moll's arrest and wait in prison before going to the gallows required four different versions of the same costume to depict the different stages of her stay – from the one in which she was taken away in through three different stages of grubbiness in jail. It is mustard cotton with a black trim, worn with a gold and black horizontal stripe silk underskirt.

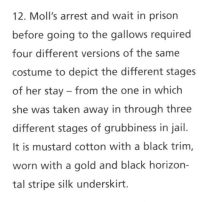

13. The final scene, showing a thirty-six-year-old Moll and Lemuel sailing to Virginia, meant a return to lighter colours. 'The dress has a slightly younger feel to it,' says Trisha, 'going away from the square neck to a round neck.' It is made of blue floral heavy cotton and worn with a plain blue quilted band underskirt and white lace fichu.

Two identical costumes were needed for Jemmy's riding outfit because actor Daniel Craig also had a stunt double. They wore a pale green longline jacket with gold trim and low pockets, a white shirt showing under the jacket sleeves, a white cotton cravat, a dark green waistcoat and tan gauntlets.

For his wedding, Jemmy wears an elaborate outfit – a longline coat with low, slit pockets, matching waistcoat, white shirt and cravat and brown breeches – that had previously been made for the film *Restoration*, but it is covered by a red velvet casaque (half-coat, half cloak) decorated with gold braid and fur trim.

In Moll's confessional scene, Jemmy wears a red velvet coat with a woven gold diamond pattern and buttons, black breeches and longline waistcoat, white cotton shirt and white lace cravat.

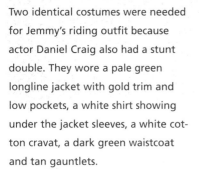

Costumes for Emily and Maria, daughters of Mayor Richardson, had to be in contrast to those of the young Moll. 'I kept the Richardson sisters in dark colours but used richer fabrics, like silks and velvets in deep burgundy and purple, to show that they were better off than Moll,' says Trisha. Emily (above, left) is pictured in a black velvet dress with ribbed taffeta trim, cream open-weave lace collar and matching cuffs, cream apron with open-weave lace, cream underskirt and off-white cotton cap. Maria is seen in a blue wool dress with black braid, off-white collar with lace edge, white cotton apron and cap, and peach and blue patterned underskirt.

The scenes in Virginia had to reflect the difference between America and Britain. 'We kept Lemuel's mother in the slightly earlier Puritan period but with a Quaker feel,' says Trisha. 'She is modestly dressed and her costumes are in sea and earth colours in natural fabrics, such as linens and woven cottons, some with lace fichu.'

Above, she is pictured in a cream and green cross-pattern dress, pale green muslin chemise, green wool shawl and fawn linen cap.

MAKE-UP AND WIGS

GRANADA'S *Moll Flanders* was a hair-raising experience for make-up designer Sue Milton. 'In a production like this,' she says, 'a lot of the work is the hair and the wigs. At the time this is set, they did wear make-up in this country, but not much, unlike a contemporary drama, where the actors have a lot on.

'Hairstyles are a guide to exactly where you are in the seventeenth century. For me, it was quite good because I was able to show Moll's journey. It also helped to make her look older as she progressed through the different husbands. I could give her different looks, depending on where she is in her story.

'My research made me understand the century a lot better. The Puritan look is very stark, not at all elaborate. Once Cromwell was gone and Charles II came to the throne, there was a remarkable new freedom, and we've been able to show that.

'Charles came back from France with his little moustache and wig, and created a new fashion. When he shaved his moustache off, men followed suit. The women of the century tended to follow the fashion of Charles's mistresses, such as Nell Gwynn.'

For the television production, Sue needed no wigs for Alex Kingston as Moll because the actress already had long, brown hair. All Sue did was to add some red to the colour to give it warmth and use fifteen hairpieces to achieve different looks. Make-up was applied mainly to age Alex from eighteen into her thirties.

At eighteen, Moll starts out with the stark look, her hair pulled back into a bun. Following the death of her first husband, Robin, she travels to London in Restoration times, sees fashionable people and immediately takes up the fashion of the time.

'We leave the bleak Puritan styles behind and meet the high Restoration era, with colour and flamboyancy,' says Sue. 'Moll wears side ringlets in her hair, which were very fashionable. It is then that she meets Dawkins, her second husband.

Make-up designer Sue Milton keeps Daniel Craig looking the part, complete with stubble.

Claire Heron was Alex Kingston's personal make-up assistant for the entire filming schedule, watched here by script supervisor Helen Moran.

'Then we move on to Moll's third husband, Lemuel, who takes her to Virginia. Here, we move into the Quaker look, back to simplicity, a result of the *Mayflower* going to America earlier in the century and taking the then current styles with it. We have four different looks for her in Virginia, depending on her age.

'While she is away, the fashion has changed and, on her return, she has the widest hairstyle, which is partly Alex's hair and partly a hairpiece. We are into high society with Moll's fourth husband, Jemmy, so we have a return to some colour.

'Moll herself moves along with these characters, depending on which husband she's with or what she's trying to portray. So, whereas in Virginia she had quite simple hairstyles, with Dawkins and Jemmy they were rather fancy.

'Moll has two fashion periods when she's with Bland, because of the time of the century, when fashionable women followed these hairstyles, which complemented the shape of the clothes. When she meets Bland on the stagecoach journey to London, her hair has a wide look to complement the sleeves of the dresses. By the time Bland dies, we have moved on and the sleeves aren't wide any more, so the hair narrows.'

As with costumes, Moll's hair and make-up had to reflect the length of her wait in Newgate Prison before going to the gallows. There were no washing facilities there, so her look deteriorates as time goes on.

'We have about seven looks for her in Newgate,' says Sue, 'ranging from that on her arrival to being a little bit dirty, then the gypsy look – going back to her roots – and, of course, she's shackled and that starts to make marks on her and she gets paler. She's been whipped, her hair is absolutely filthy and she's not been able to wash.

'Sometimes, the look depends on how she's feeling inside. For instance, she brightens up when Jemmy arrives at Newgate because there's something to live for. The sparkle is brought back, which we achieve by making up around the eyes. When she's allowed to see Jemmy, she tidies herself up a little bit.

'We clean her up for when she goes off to be hanged. Prisoners were allowed to dress in their best clothes for executions, so she would have wiped herself and made herself look more presentable.'

Diana Rigg, in the role of Lemuel's mother, is given a very simple Quaker look for her scenes, set in Virginia. A hairpiece is used and she wears Quaker caps, but make-up is applied to give her face a very colourful look.

Men's hair, like men's fashions, changed throughout the century. It started short in Puritan times, when men were renowned for their facial hair, normally little 'goatee' beards. In the Restoration era, their hair became longer, they started wearing wigs and tended to have less facial hair. For *Moll Flanders*, most of the actors wear wigs.

Christopher Fulford, who plays Dawkins, Moll's second husband, wanted his character to be flamboyant. He has more make-up than anyone else, bows in his hair, patches and lipstick. 'Chris gets the full make-up to *look* made up,' says Sue. 'After the Restoration, we could have had everyone in patches, but I thought that would be wrong. If everybody were too made up, viewers wouldn't be watching the story.'

In gaol, Alex Kingston has seven different make-up looks to show her stages of deterioration.

Moll's first lover, Rowland, is also seen towards the end of the story when Moll is in prison. 'By then,' says Sue, 'he is a mature man who is Mayor of Colchester, wealthy and very fashionable. He has his Marlborough wig and make-up.' Jemmy is seen across a period of time, so Sue's make-up is primarily to give the impression of ageing. Actor Daniel Craig wore two wigs.

John Savident, playing the clergyman travelling with Moll on her stagecoach journey to London when they are held up by Jemmy, is usually seen on screen with very little hair. For *Moll Flanders*, he wears a wig.

'When deciding what to do with an actor,' says Sue, 'you work out which period he is seen in and look at the role he is playing. Then you ask yourself whether he would be fashionable or not, then think how old he is and whether you're trying to make him look older or younger.

'With John, we had a wig that was meant to represent his own hair. I wanted to make him look different from how we normally see him on television. The fashion for men then was quite long hair. The character doesn't actually have very long hair for the time – he is a bit old-fashioned.'

By the time Rowland reappears towards the end of the story, bribing the Gaoler so that he can see Moll in private, he is Mayor of Colchester, complete with Marlborough wig and make-up.

CHAPTER SIX

FILMING

BEFORE THE FILMING of *Moll Flanders* began, director David Attwood and his crew spent a week on a recce, travelling to all the locations and working out how they wanted to shoot everything. It was at this stage that director of photography Ivan Strasburg started work on the production. 'The director of photography is responsible for the final look of the film and creating an atmosphere whereby the story is told as well as possible,' he says. 'If you're doing a big feature film with a lot of money, it's nice to come in very early and go round the locations quietly by yourself and plan things. But in television you go on a recce with the crew, which we did for *Moll* two weeks before we started shooting.

'I was able to work out, for instance, where the lights should go and what scaffolding towers would have to be built in some places. Every now and then, you know that the equipment you have available will not be enough for what you need on a particular location, so on that day you will need to order extra equipment. You also decide what is the best time of day to film a particular scene with relation to the position of the sun. The problem is that you might do the recce in beautiful weather but, when you come to film, it is overcast or even raining.'

The following week, the actors rehearsed in a basement at The Synagogue, in Dean Street, in London's West End, and the ten-week shoot began at Castle Lodge, in Ludlow, Shropshire, on 19 March 1996. It had, in fact, been due to start two days earlier, but there were problems with the location, and that filming was rescheduled for later in the shoot. 'For me, putting everything back two days was good,' says David Attwood. 'On the first day of the original schedule, it would have involved Alex Kingston as Moll sleeping with Rowland *and* Robin. To do two sex scenes with two people she'd only just met would have been extremely bad. Fortunately, that didn't happen and we started off in Ludlow.'

Where possible, the schedule was arranged to fit in with the chronological order of the story, and the first location, Ludlow – which was the setting for the Richardson family's Colchester house, featured in the early part of the story – gave the actors and crew a chance to ease their way into the production in the same way that viewers would later.

It was in Ludlow that cast and crew assembled on that March morning to start shooting *Moll Flanders*. 'The actors and actresses had stayed there overnight to acclimatise themselves to the house, whereas the crew

OPPOSITE: Director David Attwood welcomed the fact that filming on the ten-week shoot was put back two days at a late stage.

Interiors of the Richardson family's house were shot at Castle Lodge.

left Manchester at 7a.m.,' says first assistant director Vinny Fahy, whose job is to carry out the director's wishes and ensure all the scenes are scheduled in the best order, with regard to costume and make-up requirements. 'The crew arrived at 10a.m., everything was unloaded and it was almost midday before we got started. We began by filming the young Richardsons and Little Moll.'

One technical problem that immediately presented itself was that windows at Castle Lodge looked out on to traffic. 'It's always nice to see through windows when you're filming inside,' says Ivan Strasburg, 'because it gives you a feeling of reality. Unfortunately, views out of the windows were very modern.' So the panes were covered in polythene on the outside to fracture the images seen through them. Traffic noise was also a potential problem to sound recordist Nick Steer, but police helped by controlling vehicles in the area.

'In story terms,' says Ivan, 'Ludlow was a problem because it was a very po-faced part of the production, less rumbustious and without the vivacity of the rest of the story. It was difficult in terms of setting the tone because it was completely different fom everything else. But, for Alex, it was probably an easy way into the whole thing because it was a much more legitimate kind of acting – there was less of the outrageous sort of acting.

'At the beginning of a shoot, you are still experimenting. As a direc-tor of photography, you work out what the actors and the director like. Alex isn't a conventionally beautiful girl, but she's very sexy-looking. We decided early on that she looked better shot from slightly above her eye-line and that her front view was better than her profile. The first time I met Alex, she said, "My biggest problem is bags under my eyes." That's not easy to light out, and every now and then we did make a few mis-takes – you can't avoid shooting the wrong angle.'

David Attwood, as director, had to set the style and pace of the pro-duction. 'There is the old danger that everyone knows it is a period drama and gives a big performance,' he says. 'But Moll is the centrifugal force around which everybody else moves, and I decided that what she

does should be the most real performance. The further you go away from that epicentre, the more outlandish the actors can be. So you have, for instance, John Savident giving a wonderful performance as a clergyman in the stagecoach on the way to London. The energy required from those actors is different. So Moll is surrounded by this comic, gregarious, mad world.'

Something that David had not predicted was the amount of time that would be lost as a result of the costumes and type of props used in a period drama of this kind. 'In *The Bill*,' he says, 'two people having a drink and one person getting up and leaving is simple. In *Moll Flanders*, when one gets up to leave, his sword could knock seven glasses off the next table. Getting the Richardson family into a coach without people holding the horses was also difficult.

'Everything moves so slowly in period drama, but it didn't in the seventeenth century. It was an age of improvements in transport, so I couldn't have the stagecoaches just trotting through the countryside — I wanted them going fast. I wanted to create the vibrancy and the modern relevance of the seventeenth century. Also, people have to be at ease in costumes. The ones we had were sexy and vibrant, much sexier than nineteenth-century costumes.

Alex Kingston as Moll is at the centre of the action, giving a 'real' performance, whereas that from actors such as John Savident, playing the clergyman on the coach held up by Jemmy, can be more outlandish and comic.

'All that takes a while to assimilate. I always thought I could speed everything up a bit, but the fact is it takes three-quarters of an hour or an hour for a costume change and energy drained away from the whole unit during that time, so we had to kick-start ourselves again. I didn't realise how draining that was going to be. It was very frustrating.'

Lighting was a critical aspect of the production, because in the seventeenth century there was only daylight or candlelight, and Ivan Strasburg's experience proved invaluable. 'I had never worked with Ivan before,' says David, 'but I had seen a lot of his work, including *Sharpe's Rifles* and *Sharpe's Eagle*. He is a wonderful landscape photographer and a photographer of period drama.

'I think I know about lighting, and yet I hadn't fully taken on board the problems associated with lighting purely by candlelight or daylight. Fortunately, Ivan *had* taken those on board. Ivan's lighting was superb, but also a very difficult and crucial thing. We weren't doing Jane Austen people chatting to one another. It wasn't normal period lighting – it was period lighting in difficult places with people having sex, for example. The lighting was such an all-consuming thing because we needed lots of little lamps.

'After a few weeks' filming, we added a camera operator, Andrew Stephen, to our crew, which was helpful because I had someone with whom I could discuss the mechanics of shooting the scene while leaving Ivan alone to concentrate on the lighting, which itself was a major number. I like lots of input and could ask Andy how he thought we should shoot something. He would just look at the frame and tell me what he thought.'

Filming inside carriages at night posed another problem. 'People didn't have light inside carriages,' says Ivan. 'In the end, we had to do it theatrically. We had lights flashing on the outside as the carriages go past certain places, to give a feeling of movement. It's the most you can hope to do.'

During the first few weeks of filming, Alex – who had come to the production straight from starring in a fringe play, without any break – was finding her way in the role of Moll. 'Starting the shoot in the Richardson household gave us all some sort of a root,' she recalls, 'and we all bonded well as a group of people. David Lascelles and David Attwood didn't want *Moll* to have totally naturalistic performances, but to have its own sort of theatricality. This was talked about a lot, but none of us fully found the measure of it until we were three or four weeks into filming.

'In Ludlow during the first week, everything was almost too serious. We didn't find the style that had been talked about and we later re-shot

some bits at Spectrum Arena. There was a great emphasis in the Ludlow scenes on Rowland taking Moll's virginity and being the great love of her life, then dumping her. Rather than use the spirit that Moll has, picking herself up, looking at the situation she's in and using it to her best advantage, I allowed the notion of the pain left by the one she loved to enter into it a bit too much. I wasn't resilient enough in the portrayal.

'When it comes to where she speaks to camera and says, "To marry without love, or starve on the street? Or sell myself to all comers as a tuppenny whore? What would *you* do?" I did it with anger because I was angry at the situation, rather than saying, "This is the situation – of course I'm going to marry Robin." I was beginning to go down the wrong path.

'But there was always humour on the set. Even at Ludlow, there was a scene where I was supposed to be lacing up Dawn McDaniel's corset in her role as one of the Richardson sisters. I pulled so hard that I ripped the corset and there was this great noise! They've actually used that take.

'Then, at Astley Hall, it was fantastic filming with Christopher

It is at the county ball at High Peaks Hall that Moll falls for Jemmy, while Mrs Seagrave and Captain O'Malley speculate about her fortune.

David Attwood indulged his love of
Westerns during the filming of Moll
and Jemmy riding at High Peaks Hall,
in reality Haddon Hall. Alex Kingston
recalls that 'everything began to gel'
during the filming at Haddon Hall,
and she felt relaxed for the first time
during the shoot.

A steep slope at Haddon Hall means it is impossible for horses to pull the stagecoach and Alex Kingston all the way up on her arrival as Moll going to the ball.

Fulford, who plays Moll's second husband, Dawkins. The first time I met him, we had to do a bedroom scene there and he was desperate to get his tackle out and shake it around in front of the camera! It was very refreshing – that was when we were all able to relax. Then we travelled to Haddon Hall and everything began to gel. We filmed Moll's wedding to Robin in a church there and buried him in the same church.

'Gub Neal, the executive producer, came up one day and I didn't know why he was there. He kept sitting at the video monitor and talking to David Attwood. I got worried because I knew David was nervous that this was becoming a production that he hadn't envisaged – too serious. I thought they were going to sack me, so I started to lose confidence in what I was doing.

'Then I had a long talk with David and Gub. I made it clear to them that they must come and talk to me about what I was doing and felt, for the first time, that I could go up to them if I wasn't sure about something and ask for help, and it would be all right. The minute I understood that, I relaxed.

'When we were doing all the dancing and choreography for the ball scene, where Moll is introduced to Jemmy, a great friend of mine from drama school, Guy Scantlebury, arrived to play Captain O'Malley. It was suddenly really nice to have an old friend on board. At the hotel where we were staying, all the cast and crew would get together in the bar. We became drinking pals and found we could have a laugh. I thought, "It's fine. Just enjoy it. You don't need to worry."'

Haddon Hall was the scene of an unexpected drama during the filming of a scene set in the Maritime Club at Chatham, where Moll meets a group of sea captains, including her third husband, Lemuel. At one end of the room was a roaring fire, which Haddon Hall gave Granada permission to light. 'We lit the fire,' recalls Stephen Fineren, the production designer, 'and the smoke got worse and worse. The whole room became thick with black smoke. It occurred to us that the chimney must be blocked. Within about fifteen minutes, we had to abandon filming.

'The curators of the hall were beside themselves — they hadn't checked the capping of the chim-

Moll marries sea captain Lemuel, one of the three weddings filmed at Hoghton Tower for *Moll Flanders*.

ney. I have never seen a room as full of thick smoke, and there were two seventeenth-century tapestries in it that must have been affected. They threw everybody out and we were unable to resume filming for more than an hour.'

Similar problems occurred in the buildings kitchens, which were transformed into a tavern for the production. 'We lit a fire there,' says Vinny Fahy, 'and dense, black smoke completely filled the room. Nothing was coming out of the chimney! Our contract stipulated that, if we weren't out by a certain time, we faced a penalty payment,

Jemmy languishes in Newgate, in reality a set at Spectrum Arena, where his and Moll's prison scenes were filmed.

but we managed to get that waived.'

It was at Haddon Hall, in a scene where Moll and Jemmy are seen riding in the grounds of the fictional High Peaks Hall, that David Attwood attempted to indulge his love of Westerns. 'I wanted them to go riding down in the river, as they do in every Western you have ever seen,' he says. 'But British rivers are too tidal and this one had a heavy current. I could hardly stand up in it, and the bottom was rough. In the end, we got them just about galloping through the water and up on the land.'

Another problem at Haddon Hall presented itself in filming the scene where Moll's stagecoach is seen arriving for the ball. A steep slope up to the main gate meant it was impossible to get the horses to pull the coach up there, so it simply had to be dragged into position. 'One of the mistakes we made,' says Ivan Strasburg, 'was not having the horse people on the recce with us, which is a lesson to be learned. Very often, you think horses and carriages can do things they can't.'

For Vinny Fahy, one memory of Haddon Hall was the distance from the car park to the building. 'It was six minutes from where our vehicles were parked to the location,' he recalls. 'If you wanted to rehearse a scene, you had to do it the night before or drag the actors away from make-up and costume. I knew what problems they were having in costume and make-up as well because they were a distance from the sets.

'By now, Alex was really getting into her character. She would lock herself into her thoughts, oblivious to anything going on around her. We had David Lascelles's daughter Emily as a stand-in to line up the shots for her at Haddon Hall. We would rehearse with Alex and use Emily for camera rehearsals. She was with us for three weeks so that Alex didn't get too tired.'

From Haddon Hall, the cast and crew moved to Hoghton Tower, near Blackburn, to film Moll's weddings to Dawkins, Lemuel and Jemmy, the courtroom scenes of both Lucy and Moll being sentenced to death, Lucy and Moll stealing a watch from a pregnant woman at a concert hall recital, and Dawkins taking Moll to an open-air theatre — a scene that was not finished there through lack of time and had to be completed at Spectrum Arena, near Warrington, during the last few days of the shoot.

'We filmed the theatre scene at Hoghton Tower at night,' says Vinny Fahy, 'and all of us got bitterly cold. The location was four minutes away from the vehicles and we had hot-water bottles and tea, soup and hot chocolate to keep everyone warm during the evening. We didn't finish until after midnight. It was a good scene, but we had a crane that was difficult to rig and Ivan was operating the camera up on it while at the same time relaying the orders for the lights to be moved.'

A week was then spent filming on the Newgate Prison sets that had been built at Spectrum Arena. Rats, pigeons, pigs, geese and hens were all used in the scenes. 'I enjoyed doing all the Newgate stuff,' recalls Alex. 'I loved being dirty and grubby! Also, that is where Moll is seen at her oldest. Because I was tired, I felt most relaxed. It was such a relief to be there as opposed to looking fresh and supposedly eighteen.'

The draper's party scene was also filmed on an interior set at Spectrum at the end of that week, and this meant the return of Christopher Fulford as Dawkins. 'Anarchy abounded when he was on the set,' says Alex. 'It was brilliant doing the party in the draper's shop because it was all completely improvised. It was all set up with extras around who had been told it was an orgy.

'I came on the set after a complete make-up change, just before the scene was about to be filmed, and was told just to go for it. Ivan was shooting it all with a hand-held camera, moving in and out of the action. Chris went wild and there was the very funny moment when I told him I thought he should drop his trousers on the table. He loved the raunchiness of it all and was lying on the table, so I went up to him, lifted up my skirt and he was completely shocked – because I was wearing no knickers!'

But filming Alex and Christopher at Packwood House, doing the scene where Moll and Dawkins walk in Vauxhall Gardens and he proposes to her, was 'a scenic disaster', according to Stephen Fineren. It was intended to have extras selling flowers and picnicking, but rain fell all day long and it was 8p.m. before filming finished. 'We filmed Moll and Dawkins coming down a path, with a painted arch in the background,' recalls Stephen. 'There was no sunlight, just rain. It looked just about all right on the wide shot, but the close-ups were unusable and had to be redone later at Spectrum Arena.'

Up to this point, the cast and crew had been travelling from Manchester for filming every day, but Packwood House was the first of a number of locations over more than two weeks of filming that

Designer Stephen Fineren's expensive transformation of Church Street, Lacock, into a realistic seventeenth-century road made headlines when it turned into a 'sea of mud'.

required them to travel around the country and stay in hotels nearby.

Unwelcome publicity for the production came when they arrived in Lacock to prepare the Colchester street scenes. 'The biggest and most expensive problem was the road covering down the metalled street,' says Stephen Fineren. 'Ideally, it should have been semi-crushed limestone and soil. In the end, we used a mixture of soil, yellow sand and limestone dust, covered to a depth of three inches, which cost us £5,500.

'Unfortunately for the residents, on the night between the laying of the road surface and the final street dressing, Lacock experienced its heaviest rainfall in years, resulting in the street turning into a "sea of mud", as national newspapers, television and radio stations described it.' Ironically, subsequent days brought burning-hot sunshine, which turned the 'sea of mud' into a rutted road of hard-baked golden earth. By the time the Granada crew moved in with forty-five extras, cattle, pigs, horses and carts, and carriages, conditions were perfect.

Messing about on the river became a worn-out joke when filming moved to Cornwall for the scenes where Moll and Lemuel leave Chatham in his ship and arrive in Virginia to be greeted by his mother. 'We picked the worst week of the year for low tides,' recalls Stephen. 'We had to build an extra 10ft projection from our jetty out into the River Fal and drop it another two feet. Unfortunately, filming for the scenes representing Virginia Harbour had to start at 4a.m. because of the tides. Three yachts were moored on the river just beyond our point and their occupants were rudely awakened by a huge JCB that was excavating the rock for us. A farmer who lived two miles away came along the following morning and said he would like to see the JCB driver!'

Time was also lost in ferrying the cast and equipment in rubber dinghies out to the *Santa Maria*, which was used as the ship in which Moll and Lemuel sail to America. 'It all takes time,' explains Vinny Fahy. 'Then, everyone has to get off the boat and into the dinghies to get to shore for lunch. It was one of the trickiest locations to film in.' After lunch, the tide had turned and the wind had changed, causing the ship to keep moving. Three anchors were needed to keep it under control.

Even more of a problem were two shipwrecks in the river and a boat full of marijuana, which had been impounded and could not be moved until Customs & Excise officers had finished with it. Because these vessels appeared in shot, they had to be removed from the pictures digitally during the editing stages later. The harbour master helped to keep other small boats and sailing dinghies away during filming.

Locations in Lincolnshire provided the setting for the rest of the Virginia scenes. 'We were lucky to have decent weather,' recalls Ivan Strasburg. 'It wasn't very warm, but it was sunny. By then, everybody was enjoying the production because of the variety of locations, and they realised they were working on something different.

'Lincolnshire provided a big landscape and we used big, wide shots for the exteriors.

Diana Rigg, playing Lemuel's mother, was probably quite intimidating for the other actors. She just wanted to do the scenes and didn't worry about how she looked. She didn't insist on any particular angle for the lighting, like some actresses do. She was very professional.'

Tides and winds cause problems for David Attwood, his cast and crew while filming Moll and Lemuel's arrival in Virginia, where they are greeted by his mother, Mrs Golightly.

Moll and Lemuel finally arrive in America.

One problem that had to be resolved hastily was the use of a hymn in two Virginia church scenes. In his script, Andrew Davies had given the words, pointed out that it was of the wrong period but liked it and asked whether we could use it anyway. 'We found during our pre-production research that they would not have sung hymns at that time in an American church at all,' says producer David Lascelles. 'They would have sung psalms. But nobody had done anything about it – everyone thought someone else had done something.

'Some of the music for the production was pre-recorded and, the night before we were supposed to film this, someone asked me, "Who's got the music?" I realised no one had done anything, then had a panicky phone call to Susie Conklin, the script editor, and we agreed that we would use words of the hymn Andrew suggested but did not know the tune.

'So I phoned Sarah Sarhandi, who with Mark Springer was writing the music for *Moll Flanders*, and asked her if we could set a psalm to music overnight. She asked what psalm we should use and I picked up a Gideon's Bible from the hotel we were staying at in Lincoln, thumbed through it and found an index of recommended passages to read for different states of mind. I looked up 'sin' or 'guilty of sin' because these were the scenes where Moll discovers she is married to her own brother, and found Psalm 51, which was really appropriate. Sarah, who was in

London, found a Bible, put this psalm to a simple tune overnight and came up the following morning.

'Meanwhile, with Lincoln being a cathedral city, we found out the tune of the hymn whose words Andrew had used and got hold of a hymn book with the music. Sarah arrived from London with a viola and conducted the members of the cast though these two pieces of music.'

When filming finished in Lincolnshire, everyone headed back for Manchester, with Granada staff returning to their homes and families each evening and freelance crew and actors staying at the Victoria & Albert Hotel, opposite the television studios, while filming for three days near Bolton and the final two weeks at Spectrum Arena.

Roddlesworth Reservoir was the setting for the 'stand and deliver' scene where Jemmy holds up a stagecoach in which Moll is travelling. The day was overcast, but the cameras started rolling every time sun appeared through the clouds. While all this was happening, two scenes of Moll and Jemmy's honeymoon coach travelling through picturesque countryside were filmed in long-shot half a mile away, directed by David Lascelles.

Extras were called for whenever necessary. Eighty, including eight children from a nearby primary school, were used at Rivington Castle,

The cameras film Jemmy's 'stand and deliver' scene every time the sun appears through the clouds on an overcast day in deepest Lancashire.

The weather is not kind to eighty extras, including a party of schoolchildren, who are taking part in the Tyburn gallows scenes, filmed at the ruined castle, Rivington.

near Bolton, where the gallows scenes for Lucy Diver and Moll were filmed. However, it was necessary to re-create a crowd of several hundred spectators, so those who were filmed on the day were multiplied on screen during the editing stage of production.

'The hangings happened only every so often in a year,' says David Attwood, 'and it was a big day out for people, an event like Pavarotti in the Park. We tried to keep that flavour. In a couple of wide shots, the extras will be digitalised to give three times the number.'

It was at Rivington that actress Nicola Walker performed her own stunt as Lucy Diver being hanged, and anyone arriving at the location

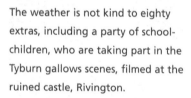

On days when large numbers of extras are taking part in filming, a second catering van is needed.

After Lucy Diver's sentence to death, actress Nicola Walker insists on doing her own hanging stunt, with the help of stunt co-ordinator Nick Powell.

ABOVE AND RIGHT: The remarks of the Fat Man (Irving Czechowicz) at Lucy's hanging lead Moll to knee him in the groin and steal his watch, but she throws it away on realising that nothing can bring Lucy back.

first thing in the morning could find her bringing a whole new meaning to the expression 'hanging around on set' as she rehearsed with stunt co-ordinator Nick Powell, who taught Mel Gibson to fight with a sword in the feature film *Braveheart* and, just before starting work on *Moll Flanders*, worked with Kenneth Branagh on *Hamlet*.

One of the extras who appeared next to Alex Kingston in the crowd

during Lucy's execution scene was Irving Czechowicz, who had a speaking role as the Fat Man shouting, 'Look at her dance! I never seen the like of it!' In the script, Moll turns around, knees him in the groin, grabs his watch after he falls in a heap on the ground and walks away at speed, only to throw the watch away on realising that it will not bring Lucy back. Irving, who had been seen on television briefly that

same week as a house landlord in *Emmerdale*, sat around on the outdoor set all morning watching other parts of the scene being filmed, before stepping into position for his moment of glory — and took a knee in the crotch twenty times during rehearsals and filming.

After Rivington and a day at nearby Smithills Hall, which was used for the courtroom scene where Moll's mother is sentenced to transportation, all that remained was two weeks on the London streets set at Spectrum Arena. This gave cast and crew the apparent luxury of being indoors in a warmer and more controlled environment, although many were soon wearing face masks to protect them from the dust that was coming up off Stephen Fineren's realistic roads.

'The problems we had were that it was dirty, smelly and dis-

ABOVE AND OPPOSITE: After being arrested for stealing, Moll finds herself sentenced at the same time as Jemmy.

Moll faces the gallows unless Jemmy can save her, but Alex Kingston finds time to laugh despite the freezing weather.

Alex Kingston clutching two
hot-water bottles to her bosom was
a familiar sight on location.

gusting,' says Ivan Strasburg. 'It was a nightmare trying to keep things
clean. Turning round the horses and carts and trying to reset them was
another nightmare.'

Although filming was extended by three days at a late stage, it was
still necessary to drop some scenes during the shoot through lack of
time. One in which Moll bribes a priest so that she can see Jemmy in his
cell at Newgate had to be rewritten with the gaoler instead of the priest

because filming was rescheduled and the actor was not available on the new shooting day.

Throughout the production, sex scenes – which can be awkward and embarrassing for the actors – proved to be no problem. 'When it came down to having to have sex all the time with all these different guys,' says Alex, 'I was so relaxed that it made them feel relaxed, too. They realised they didn't need to be nervous or embarrassed, and we all had a giggle. When you're in such close proximity to somebody and can have a laugh, you become good mates. I hadn't met Daniel Craig before, but he was absolutely brilliant. We just got on really well and found that we were really good friends.'

Vinny Fahy reveals that he also tried to make the environment on set more comfortable for the sex scenes. 'I tried to keep some of the crew away and put more women on the set from costume and make-up as a confidence-booster,' he says. 'But Alex handled it very professionally.'

More worrying for Alex was the gruelling schedule that involved her in almost every scene, with endless costume changes. The actress wrapping herself in a quilt and clutching two hot-water bottles to her bosom was a common sight between takes on location.

'I do have a lot of stamina,' she says, 'but early on David Lascelles's daughter Emily had time off from university and came out for three or four weeks to look after me. Corsets are very restrictive and the dresses were incredibly heavy. I had up to four or five costume, make-up and hairpiece changes a day. It would have been a nightmare if I had worn wigs because I would have needed new bald caps stuck on every time and that would have taken even longer.

'My lowest point was on the day we filmed Moll's gallows scene at Rivington Castle. It was freezing after lunch and, at one time, sleet was falling. I was wearing a flimsy ballgown and the cold had got so into my bones that no number of hot-water bottles could warm me up. When I spoke to camera at the end of the day, I thought I wouldn't be able to get my lines out because I was shivering so much. I got a chest infection after that and was so run down by then.'

But worse was to come when Alex collapsed on set at Spectrum Arena a day before the end of filming. This came after she had to put on a corset for a prison scene where Moll's shackles are taken off for her to go on the tumbril on her way to the gallows. 'I was so exhausted, I was standing and fainted,' she recalls. 'I was completely out. I was pleased when filming came to an end, but at the same time, you don't want it to end. I will never forget this production. I'm sure I'll never work so hard again in my life.'

CHAPTER SEVEN

POST-PRODUCTION

A T THE END OF EVERY day's filming, the 'rushes' were sent back to Granada Television's studios in Manchester and subsequently transferred on to videotape, with all 'takes' given a consistent quality in terms of look and lighting so that everything would be ready at the end of the shoot for David Attwood to piece *Moll Flanders* together into four hours of television with editor Edward Mansell, who had previously worked with him on an episode in the Granada series *Made in Heaven*.

Throughout the filming, producer David Lascelles kept an eye on the rushes and gave feedback to the director. 'My role was to support him,' says David. 'The aim of a producer is to enable the director to make as good a film as possible. My theory of film production is that, in an ideal world, the producer should be able to go on holiday on the first day of the shoot. If you've set it all up right, cast it right and crewed it right, and got the right schedule, you should be able to look at the rushes and phone your comments through, but I've never worked on a production where that's possible.

'I spoke to David regularly and acted as a key sounding board about the way things were going to be done. We really could have done with a longer pre-production period. As a result, a lot of decisions were having to be made on the hoof. There were even bits and pieces of casting that had not been done when we started. Also, I had to keep an eye on the financial and administrative side, ensuring that the money was being spent in the right way, and deciding whether we could afford a particular piece of equipment and how to reallocate money saved in one area to another.'

Two days after filming finished, Alex Kingston went into a studio with David Attwood to record her voiceovers. Once that day's work had ended, her part in the production was over. Then David started work on the editing, and at this point, made a momentous decision – he changed the end of Episode 1.

Originally, as written by Andrew Davies, that episode finished with Moll leaving Colchester and Puritan times and arriving in London at the start of the Restoration era. David decided to bring part of that colour-

Director David Attwood decided after filming was over to include Moll's marriage to Daniel Dawkins in Episode 1, moving the story on from Puritan times into the Restoration era.

The scene in which Mrs Seagrave (Trevyn McDowell) introduces Moll to Jemmy originally ended Episode 2, but David Attwood progressed the story up to his marriage proposal.

ful period into the first hour to show the changing times and give an idea of what was to come, which was distinctly different from Moll's upbringing in the country.

'I always knew there was a possibility that I might move Dawkins into Episode 1,' explains David. 'You have to acknowledge that the script is not the be all and end all. You make sure when you are filming that you leave yourself those options.

'Episode 1 was all set in one place. You're trying to establish a believable character with whom the audience can identify, so you have to know where she's coming from, and you have to take time to do that. But, after finishing filming, I decided to put the Dawkins section in that episode.

'I felt we had sufficiently established Moll as a character we wanted to engage with but we wanted to move the story along. So she goes to London and meets Dawkins, and we establish the picaresque, rompish nature of the story. The episode finishes with Dawkins setting off for France and Moll going into the Mint.

'Episode 2 then begins with her going to Chatham and goes on to tell the whole story of her life in Virginia, which works wonderfully well. Originally, that episode finished with Moll back in England and being introduced to Jemmy by Mrs Seagrave at High Peaks Hall. That seemed to me to be a bit of a problem that you have seen him, he says, "Delighted," and the episode ends. I'm not sure, as a viewer, that's enough to take you on to Episode 3, because you have to know what's going to happen, so we've taken Episode 2 as far as Jemmy proposing marriage. We didn't have to adjust the last two episodes because we were over time on them.'

Moll Flanders was made as four episodes, each with two commercial breaks, although WGBH of Boston, which had already agreed to buy the programme, wanted to show it as two two-hour episodes, so it was also edited into that form by David and Edward. When David Attwood and David Lascelles presented the first two hours to executive producer Gub

Neal to view, there was debate about whether it should be screened in this way in Britain, too, but it was finally decided to keep it as four one-hour episodes. Also, David Attwood saw the commercial breaks as a distinct advantage. 'They force you to acknowledge the three-act structure,' he says. 'Andrew Davies did include breaks in his script, but I have had to change them in Episodes 1 and 2.'

One element of the creative process that was still not completed when David and Edward set about editing the programme was the music. Any music that was a part of the actual scenes was pre-recorded, reflecting the instruments that were played during the seventeenth century, and used during the filming, whereas the rest of the production's music was scored afterwards by Mark Springer and Sarah Sarhandi, who gave that more of a modern feel.

'For some of the scenes set at weddings or in taverns, they wanted music of the period that had to be pre-recorded,' says Mark. 'So we looked at groups around London who play contemporary music, like Purcell and country dances. We auditioned some of these people and decided to use The Broadside Band, which features Jeremy Barlow, who plays the spinet and is their musical director. We also spoke to the choreographer, Carolyn Choa, about the tempo of dances and worked out what would be the right pieces.'

After pre-recording the 'live' music, there was a gap of several months before Mark and Sarah composed that which would be played over scenes. This was because *Moll Flanders* had to be filmed before they could see the result and get to work on their score. 'We went on location to get the feel of it,' says Mark, 'and we also went to the Granada studios to see a rough cut. Although it's set in the seventeenth century, it's a very contemporary tale – it could be now.'

Like the initial ambitions of the producer and director, the aim was to be different. 'People who like period drama and regularly watch it will switch on *Moll Flanders* and probably get quite a shock,' says David Attwood. 'I can't guess how they will respond to that shock, but I hope they will recognise that it's different and go with it. We are trying to attract the people who haven't watched period drama before who might go "Wow!"'